LIVES OF EMINENT AFRICANS

BY

G. A. GOLLOCK

AUTHOR OF "SONS OF AFRICA," ETC.

WITH 5 PORTRAITS AND 2 MAPS

NEGRO UNIVERSITIES PRESS
NEW YORK

Originally published in 1928
by Longmans, Green and Co. Ltd., London

Reprinted 1969 by
Negro Universities Press
A DIVISION OF GREENWOOD PUBLISHING CORP.
NEW YORK

SBN 8371-2062-4

PRINTED IN UNITED STATES OF AMERICA

TO

MY FRIEND

JAMES EMMAN KWEGYIR AGGREY

WHO TAUGHT THE PEOPLE OF THREE CONTINENTS
TO UNDERSTAND ONE ANOTHER

PREFACE

THIS book has been written for young Africans stepping out into life or in their final year in college or training school.

Throughout the world, as in Africa, the new generations are facing changed conditions and paths untrodden before. They need not only good friends beside them, but light from the records of their race. To see how one's forefathers met new situations, to discern the qualities which led to success, the mistakes which brought disaster, is singularly worth while.

It is evident from the stories that follow that young Africans have a racial heritage of which they may be justly proud. For every story here told, ten more could be written, equally full of human interest, equally rich in suggestion for life to-day.

Thanks for help are due to administrators and other officials, to teachers in government and mission schools in all parts of Africa, to leaders of mission boards with work in Africa, and to the librarian and staff of the splendid library of the Royal Colonial Institute in London. A few special acknowledgments must find place. To Canon Phelps Stokes and to Dr. T. Jesse Jones, of Washington and New York, is due the initial action which brought the writing of this book within the generous interest of the Phelps-Stokes Trustees. To Dr. Loram, one of the Commissioners of Native Affairs in South Africa, the book owes its title and the general scheme of its contents ; the earlier chapters gained from his expert editing, and his suggestions ranged over them all. The Rev. E. W. Smith, formerly of Northern Rhodesia, author of *The Golden Stool* and other

v

works, has given counsel throughout, and read the final
MS. A like kindly office was undertaken at the end by
Captain James Stuart, formerly Assistant Native Commissioner in Natal. The aid given by several Africans,
and notably by Dr. Aggrey, has been of unique value.
The key of personal friendship with him has opened the
way to an understanding of the life and thought of other
great Africans.

The design on the cover is from a freehand drawing
by a woman of the Aro tribe, living not far from the
district of Chief Onoyom (p. 132). It was lent by Mrs.
Arnot, of the Mary Slessor Memorial Home.

Every care has been taken to secure accuracy in the
facts recorded, but the available authorities vary so often
that some of their statements cannot be reconciled.
Except for such difference in detail, the stories are
literally true and uncoloured.

G. A. G.

TABLE OF CONTENTS

LIST OF ILLUSTRATIONS

MAP OF AFRICA

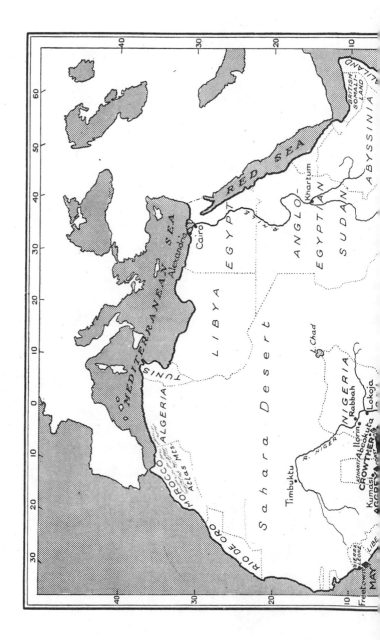

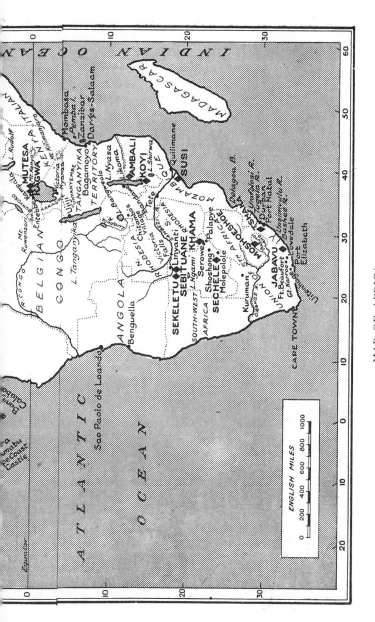

MAP OF AFRICA

(A diamond ◆ shows where the "Eminent Africans" lived.)

LIVES OF EMINENT AFRICANS

TSHAKA, THE ZULU WARRIOR-KING

A Restless Boy

BETWEEN three and four hundred years ago there was a great migration of tribes from the centre of Africa towards the south. Some of them moved slowly and made long pauses here and there. Those were the tribes who lived by tilling the ground. Others moved more quickly and seldom stayed long in one place. These were the pastoral tribes who owned great flocks and herds. The cattle soon ate up all the green food in a neighbourhood and had to be driven on to new pastures.

Among the pastoral tribes was one called Zulu, after the name of their first chief. It settled in the basin of the White Umfolosi river, in what is now Natal. The Zulus were fine men, intelligent and brave, but the tribe was little known. The chief of the powerful Mtetwa tribe, north of the Tugela river, was their feudal lord.

About the year 1786, when Senzangakona was chief of the Zulus, a son was born to him who was to strike terror through great regions of South Africa. His mother Nandi, the chief's favourite wife, was daughter of the chief of the Langeni clan.

When Tshaka, as the baby boy was called, was one year old, Nandi took him to her parents' house to be weaned ; this was a custom among the Zulus. There Tshaka stayed till he passed from childhood into boyhood. Then his father

1

came to see him and give him the loin-covering which was
worn by elder boys and men. But Tshaka was wild and
reckless. It is told in an old story current among the Zulus
that he behaved disgracefully to his father. Senzangakona
was washing himself in the cattle kraal in the presence of his
counsellors, when Tshaka jumped over him. The son's
shadow fell upon the father, and it was believed that this
caused the chief to be always ailing until the day of his
early death.

Tshaka also refused to receive the loin-covering from his
father. He made his relations so angry that his life was in
danger. He fled naked, and dare not return to the Langeni.
He had become most unpopular during his stay.

The mother stood by her troublesome boy. It is a way
that mothers have. She advised him to go to the chief out
of whose house her mother—Tshaka's grandmother—came.
But soon he had to flee from there for he set every one
against him again.

At last, probably through the plans of his mother who
loved him, Tshaka found a friend. Dingiswayo, chief of the
Mtetwa tribe, saw that the troublesome lad had fine qualities.
He presented him with the loin-covering and enrolled him as
a soldier in his army.

What was Nandi to do? She was still the favourite
wife of her husband, and had the little world in which she
lived at her feet. But Tshaka was driven out and she could
not do without her son. For his sake, and against her
husband's will, she gave up wealth and position and went to
join her boy. She believed in his future greatness; she
thought everybody had turned against him; mother love
brought her to his side.

The Story of Dingiswayo

Who was the man whom Tshaka was willing to follow?
What was the story of his life? He, too, had had troubles
at home. As he grew towards manhood Dingiswayo found
that his father Jobe, chief of the Mtetwa, suspected him.
The chief, thinking his elder sons were going to rebel against

him, told the executioners to put them to death. With great difficulty, and with the assistance of one of his sisters, Dingiswayo managed to escape. He remained in exile till his father died. He got the name of Dingiswayo or the Wanderer.

When news reached him that Jobe was dead he sent word that he was coming back to be chief. There were rumours that he would come on a swift, strong, beautiful animal such as the tribe had never seen. He arrived riding on a horse and was hailed as the new chief. He at once began to teach the Mtetwa to fight in a new way. He had learned a great deal about war while he was away.

One story says he had gone southward to the borders of Cape Colony and seen a Boer commando being drilled. Another and more likely story says that he went to the great Chief Bungane, head of the mighty Hlubi tribe in the Wakkerstroom territory. It is said that there were three Englishmen at Bungane's kraal; the Hlubi called them *izinkau*—monkeys. With one of these men Dingiswayo made special friends. They talked of the white men's armies and their ways of war. A horse and firearms were given to Dingiswayo. The Englishman seems to have gone back with Dingiswayo, but was murdered by the Qwake tribe before reaching that of the Mtetwa.

Tshaka had his first taste of success in Dingiswayo's kraal. Like most boys he came to an age when he wanted to be friends with people instead of angering them and going off alone. He soon began to be popular, for he was brave and strong and handsome. People liked him because he could make songs and dance and jest.

Tshaka knew, of course, how African tribes made war. They rushed with their chiefs into battle and fought fiercely. Each man knew how to use his own weapon, but there was no order in their advance. There were no words of command which every warrior obeyed. But Dingiswayo had changed all that. He put into practice what he had learned from his English friend. Tshaka soon learned the new way of fighting. He was quick to see how it could be improved. He rose from rank to rank in the Mtetwa army till he became a favourite leader. But no one realised yet how ·much suffering was to flood South Africa through Tshaka's genius for war.

In 1810 Senzangakona died, and Dingiswayo helped Tshaka to become chief of the Zulus. The two men, one chief of the big Mtetwa tribe, the other chief of the smaller Zulu tribe, were friends and their warriors fought together. But about two years later Dingiswayo stupidly allowed himself to be captured by his rival, who afterwards put him to death. Then the Mtetwa tribe, who already knew Tshaka as one of their leaders in battle, put themselves and their great army under the Zulu chief. They took the Zulu name. This was the beginning of the greatness of the Zulu people.

How Tshaka made the Zulus Great

Even among the Zulu warriors Tshaka looked like a chief. He was now about twenty-four years of age. His height was over six feet. His limbs were well-formed and his body disciplined by exercise. His strength and agility were the pride of the tribe. He could walk longer distances than any of his warriors. The Zulus, who never liked a chief with a wrinkle or a grey hair, had a leader such as they desired. Tshaka loved power and was born to command men. His mind was as vigorous as his body. But his actions already showed that he lacked the moral qualities which make a strong man good.

The Zulus being a pastoral people wanted more cattle, always more cattle, and the cattle needed more land on which to graze. In a country where many tribes lived close together cattle and land could only be got by war. Tshaka paid no attention to the arts of peace, but turned his attention to the army. Dingiswayo had already shown him how to make it strong. The army was divided into regiments— or butos—each containing men of about the same age. One buto had men aged from thirty-five to forty, another men from forty to forty-five, and so on. Each regiment was shut up in a military kraal, where they were provided with beef

TSHAKA, THE ZULU WARRIOR-KING.

from the cattle taken in war and corn grown and prepared by the women. A soldier was seldom allowed to have a wife of his own. Tshaka was determined that they should think only of war. As soon as a youth was old enough to bear a shield he had to join the army. He was put into the kraal of his regiment and had no companions but soldiers. Later on Tshaka strengthened his army by adding to it the finest boys and some of the ablest men from the conquered tribes.

If they did not choose to become his warriors the boys were kept to carry burdens and the men were killed.

The warriors had long and severe training on the parade ground. When the Chief reviewed them it was a terrible time. An order would be given which meant death to hundreds of soldiers. If one regiment hesitated for a moment to obey it another was ready to cut the cowards down. Each regiment was jealous of the rest.

The Zulus had oval shields made of ox-hide which were large enough to conceal their bodies. The regiments had different-coloured shields. They differed not only in colour but in the pattern they bore. Great warriors had white shields with one or two black spots; the shields of the young warriors were black; the shields of married men were red.

Tshaka invented a new and deadly weapon for the warriors. It was a short-handled, long-bladed assegai which could either cut or stab, but not be thrown. He also arranged a new order of battle. The amabuto were spread out in a semicircle or great crescent. The ends were called the horns and the central body the chest. Behind the centre of the crescent a body of warriors waited to see where the battle would need them most. A great horror of the Zulu impis and of the horns which closed round their enemies soon fell upon scores of tribes in fair Natal and beyond it.

What Dingiswayo had begun Tshaka completed. It was through this great force of fighting-men that Tshaka meant to make himself and the Zulus great. But the true greatness of a ruler or of his people is not found in war. Greatness is the fruit of liberty, security and happiness at home. Before we follow Tshaka's armies, let us see the Chief in the midst of his own tribe.

TSHAKA AT HOME

Tshaka had beautiful places to live in. A traveller described the distant view of one of his kraals. It was a great enclosure about three miles round, on raised ground in the midst of lovely scenery, with deep ravines and lofty timber. But Tshaka had no real home. In his kraals there were many girls and women, but he gave no woman the place of wife. No baby son born to him was allowed to live lest when he grew up he might kill his father and make himself chief.

Nandi, who had given up everything for her son in his restless boyhood, had a place of high honour now that he was chief. She had her own residence and officials and servants. Tshaka gave her an exalted position ; she was the only person in the world he was prepared to trust. As for her, she loved no one but her son. Occasionally there were sharp differences between them and even violent scenes. The trouble came because Tshaka was determined to have no legal wife, and Nandi wanted to see an heir to her mighty dynasty. Both mother and son were passionate and obstinate. But except on that one point their relations were good.

Tshaka's people cowered before him because the glance of his eye might mean death. He ruled them not by love but by fear. Yet sometimes he would dance with them for hours, exercising his splendid strength. Here is a description of Tshaka dancing which a white man wrote :

The Zulus formed a half-circle, the men in the centre, the boys at the sides. The king placed himself in the middle of the space within the circle, and hundreds of girls stood opposite to the men, three deep, in a straight line. The Chief began to dance, the warriors followed, the girls kept time by singing, clapping their hands, and raising their bodies on their toes. The strange attitudes of the men exceeded anything I ever saw before. The Chief was remarkable for his unequalled agility and the surprising

muscular power he exhibited. He was decorated with a pro-
fusion of green and yellow glass beads. The ceremony was
performed with great regularity, Tshaka setting time for every
motion. Wherever he cast his eye the greatest effort was made.
Nothing could exceed the exertion of the whole party until
sunset. Then Tshaka and the girls retired into the palace :
some of the warriors went to their huts, others to wash in the
river.

There were white officials and missionaries in other parts
of South Africa, but none of them found their way to
Tshaka's kraals. A few adventurous white traders, however,
entered his country and lived there for years. Here is the
story of these men.

The Story of the Adventurous Traders

The traders came up the east coast from Cape Town, hoping
to find a way to get inland in Natal. Misfortune dogged them
from the first. Three times the little ships in which they sailed
were lost. Things were no better on land than on sea. It was
a wild adventure indeed. The country was rich and full of
elephants. In Natal proper, the inhabitants were few, but as
Tshaka the dread Zulu warrior claimed the territory as his own,
to Tshaka the traders must go.

So in July, 1824, a little group of adventurers led by an
English sailor and the son of a hotel keeper in Cape Town, named
Henry Fynn, arrived at Tshaka's royal military kraal. They
were the first white men he had seen. He was the first great
African they had met. They were polite to each other. The
visitors soon returned to their settlement, leaving Henry Fynn
behind. Then the luck of the white men turned. Two days
later when Tshaka was dancing with his people a sudden attempt
was made on his life. He was severely wounded. But Fynn
was able to dress the wound and save the chief's life. Henceforth
Tshaka was more or less the white man's friend.

He gave the traders a grant of land, including the port of
Natal and the islands and some surrounding country. The
traders became like tribal chiefs. Three or four hundred miserable people, often famishing, lived in the territory round Port
Natal. When other tribes were destroyed in warfare the refugees
often took shelter with the white men until at last they had about

5,000 under their care. Tshaka never allowed the white men to trade with his subjects. All buying and selling had to be done with him. The traders gave him presents ; he gave them ivory and cattle in return. Tshaka was not easy to please. When he grew angry their lives were often in peril. He occasionally forced them to join in his wars. When they visited him in his kraal they did not always find him dancing with his people ; they had to witness cruelty which it was horrible to behold.

The white men wore out their clothes and their shoes and could not buy more. They were ashamed to be seen by other white men. It was a wild, half-civilised life. At last they quarrelled among themselves. Some time after Tshaka's death, in consequence of the hostile attitude taken by Dingana towards them, they broke up their settlement and, all but one of them, temporarily left Natal (1834).

There was one present for which Tshaka asked the white men again and again. Though he could neither read nor write he had a keen intelligence and never forgot anything he heard. When the traders first came he inquired about the king of England. Was he as handsome as Tshaka ? The traders could truly say that he—King George the Fourth—was not. Had he many soldiers in his army ? Yes, he had. Did he look old ? Had he white hair ? One of the traders idly told him that in England they had a medicine which made white hair black again. It forthwith became a passion of Tshaka's life to get that medicine from over the sea. We know that the Zulus did not want a chief with white hair.

Tshaka dealt out death to all round him when his mood was bad. He seemed like a giant without reason, a being with passions beyond those of an ordinary man. The ferocity of Tshaka to his own people is too terrible to describe. One of his kraals bore a name which means " drive-the-old-people-out." All old men in the kraal had been murdered by Tshaka's orders because they could no longer fight.

The unrestrained cruelty of Tshaka reached its height when Nandi his mother died. The whole tribe was in duty bound to assemble at the Chief's kraal to mourn for her. Here the most appalling scenes were enacted, for the

Zulus began to kill one another. Fynn, who was an eye-witness, says that seven thousand were killed in the royal kraal alone. Those, moreover, who failed to attend were killed. Parties of soldiers were sent out in all directions, by order of the Chief, and no doubt hundreds more were slain. The slaughter went on for a fortnight. Tshaka mourned truly for his mother, but he had a special purpose in what he did, he wanted to strike terror into the people. This was too much even for Zulu warriors to bear. The massacre on the death of his mother broke Tshaka's power as Chief.

Tshaka at War

It is easy to see that war would be very terrible when Tshaka was in command of the army he had trained. We recall the discipline of the regiments, the great shields which protected the warriors, the deadly power of the stabbing assegais with which they armed themselves, the order of their battle array. Tshaka was ruthless to his own Zulus ; he was more ruthless to his foes. History tells of monsters of cruelty, like Nero the Roman Emperor who gloated over the suffering he inflicted on his own people. History tells also of great soldiers like Napoleon, Emperor of France, who sacrificed every one for the sake of victory and swept over land after land. But history tells of few men, who, like Tshaka, were terrible both at home and abroad. He is called the Nero of the Zulus and the Black Napoleon.

Tshaka raided first north-west, then south-west and south, then due north, bringing ruin to one tribe after another. The terror of the Zulu armies was carried far and wide. The fierce impis arrived, fought, conquered, slew their enemies, seized the cattle, burned the kraals, murdered old men, women, and children, took with them the finest boys and most beautiful girls—and went on to the next tribe. By 1820 Tshaka had left large regions without inhabitants and made South Africa ring with his name. By 1824, when the first white man arrived on the scene, there was utter desolation between the Tugela and Umzim-vubu (St. John) rivers. The few broken tribes left were starving, Tshaka was undisputed master of the whole of Natal. It was bad enough that Tshaka should ravage the fair fields of Natal and then take his armies elsewhere. But there was far worse in store. The whole country, we are told, seemed like an ocean in a storm, the inhabitants being like waves rolling backwards and forwards carrying ruin and misery. Tshaka's trusted general Umziligazi (Moselekatse) broke away and crossed the Drakensberg into what is now the Transvaal, fighting as he went. He took many impis with him and formed the fierce Matabele power. Another general, Zwangendaba, revolted and fought his way northward. He built up the warlike Angoni. The tribes as they fled from the Zulus became almost as terrible as the Zulus themselves. They joined together as they tried to escape and worked havoc where they went.

A well-known writer, S. M. Molema, himself a member of a Bantu tribe, sums up Tshaka's wars in these words : "Thus carrying fire and sword into the surrounding countries, putting to flight and confusion the neighbouring tribes, butchering both friend and foe alike as it pleased his whim, . . . Tshaka had in a quarter of a century destroyed altogether some million souls or so, rendered barren and desolate districts formerly fertile and populous, and had inscribed for himself in blood a name in history."

We come back once more to Tshaka in his kraal, the white traders passing to and fro. The Chief's position is not what it was before. The Zulus begin to be sated with blood. His armies which once swept the country have met with defeat near Delagoa Bay, and, with their numbers reduced by about half, returned half-starving and stricken with disease. Tshaka's thoughts went often to the white men in the south who had come across the sea. Their king, he thought, was such a man as himself. So he sent an embassy to the Government at Cape Town, not knowing what he wanted to effect. He made a vague offer to destroy all the tribes along the frontier, if the white men wished it to be done.

Tshaka's envoys got no further than Port Elizabeth.

His three *indunas*, one of whom was a white man, had been given no specific message except that Tshaka was desirous of concluding a treaty of amity with the British people. Tshaka could not write himself. The Government would not let the white trader in the party speak in the name of the great Chief, though, as a matter of fact, he had been specially appointed to do so. So the indunas were sent back in a warship from Port Elizabeth, with courteous words. Tshaka was dissatisfied with their reception by the officials and sent a second embassy with different people in it, this time overland.

While waiting for their return, Tshaka sent an army to destroy the Pondos ; he plundered them of everything, but the chief and people managed to hide till the Zulus went away. He also prepared an army to attack the Ama-Tembu and Ama-Xosa and sent it as far as the Bashee river. But the Englishman, Henry Fynn, who had saved Tshaka's life years before, was with him and persuaded the Chief to recall the army and await the return of his embassy. The British Government, he said, might wish to protect the tribes Tshaka purposed to destroy.

Tshaka's indunas got safely to Cape Town and were well received. But again they could not make the object of their visit clear. An officer of the Cape Mounted Rifles was ordered to go back with them to confer with the Chief himself. But tidings came which stopped the journey before it was begun.

Tshaka's Death

Was Tshaka ever afraid ? Three incidents in his story give an answer to the question. Why did he allow no son of his to live ? Why did he want to make white hair black ? Why did he kill so many when his mother died ? Because he feared. Sons might rise up against their father. White hairs might make the Zulus want to have done with a Chief who was growing old. The killing when Nandi died was meant to show the awful consequences of death in the kraal of the Chief. Tshaka was afraid of a violent death. What he feared came. The Zulus were sick of the massacres at home and discouraged by their recent defeat in war. Tshaka had no sons to wrest the chieftainship from him, but he forgot that his brothers might aspire to sit in his place.

One evening in September, 1828, Tshaka sat in his military kraal Dukuza, near the Umvoti river about fifty miles from Port Natal. Two or three chieftains were with him watching the great droves of cattle being driven into the safety of the kraal before night fell. Mbopa, a trusted servant of Tshaka's, came up suddenly with a spear used for killing cattle in his hand and spoke rudely to the chiefs. Tshaka's companions sprang up to seize him, for things like that were not done without punishment in the kraal. In a moment two of Tshaka's half-brothers crept up behind him, while his attention was fixed on Mbopa, and one of them— Mhlangana (aided and abetted by Dingana)—stabbed the Chief in the back. Tshaka dropped his blanket and tried to escape. They overtook him, and though he cried for mercy and offered to be their servant, his brothers stabbed him further and Mbopa gave him his death-blow with the cattle spear. Then they danced round his body as hunters do when they have slain their prey. There is a story that no hyena touched the dead body of the dreaded Tshaka, though it lay on the ground all through the night.

Dingana, one of the half-brothers who had murdered Tshaka, succeeded him as chief. After him Mpande, another half-brother, ruled. Cetshwayo, son of Mpande, became chief while his father still lived. He was succeeded by his son Dinuzulu, who died in 1913.

MOSHOESHOE, THE CHIEF OF THE MOUNTAIN

I T is worth while to watch anything grow. A plant puts out leaves and blossoms ; a tree spreads its branches ; a calf grows great and develops horns ; a boy becomes a man and a girl a woman. But this chapter is the story of something even greater—the growing up of a nation. For Moshoeshoe [1] was the first chief of the Basuto. To follow his story is to see a nation grow.

THE MAKING OF A CHIEF

Moshoeshoe was born at the close of the eighteenth century at Monkhoaheng on the Thlotsi river. His father was a hunter, chief of a village of the Bamokoteli tribe. Moshoeshoe was bright and strong, a leader among the village boys. He went in due time to the initiation school. When he came out his grandfather Peete took him to see a cousin named Mohlomi, then growing old. Sometimes an hour with a good man shapes a whole life. The meeting of Moshoeshoe and Mohlomi was such a time. This is the story of Mohlomi.

The Story of Mohlomi

In the history of every nation now and again a figure stands out suddenly, towering above the rest. At a time when South Africa was full of struggle and confusion Mohlomi, son of Monyane, was such a man. His early life was like that of his companions. When he came to be chief of his father's clan he was kind and just and friendly. He never quarrelled. He ruled his people

---

[1] The name is frequently spelled " Moshesh."

14

with fairness and judged wisely in questions he had to decide. He made no war. He relieved the distressed. He loved children. Mohlomi ate little and drank only water and milk. He had great fame as a healer and knew many powerful cures. But he had no belief in witchcraft and he never "threw the bones" when he wanted to find out secret things. He liked to expose the witchdoctors. One day he was making shields and hid one in a secret place. He called in the diviners to find it. The people were looking on. The diviners threw the bones, and charged one person after another with the theft. At last Mohlomi brought the shield out of its hiding-place where he had put it himself; the diviners looked very foolish, and Mohlomi urged the people never to believe in them again.

Mohlomi was a great traveller. At a time when all the chiefs distrusted one another, and men were afraid to stir from the shelter of their tribe, he found honour and welcome everywhere. People flocked to listen to his words. Chiefs on the verge of war laid their plans before him. Mohlomi counselled them to love peace. "It is better," he said, "to thresh corn than to sharpen the spear."

In his mind and spirit Mohlomi belonged to a wider world. He was born with greatness in his soul. Long years after his death his wife (Moliepollo) said that in the initiation school when his companions were asleep the boy had communion with heaven. He believed that one night he was caught up to the skies and heard a voice saying to him, "Go, rule by love and look on the people as men and brothers."

For his dignity, his wisdom, and his love of peace the name of Mohlomi is still revered in Basutoland.

To this noble old man young Moshoeshoe was brought. Already the lad was eager for greatness. Brushing his forehead against that of the boy, as a token that he blessed him, Mohlomi took off one of his own long ear-rings, and fastened it in Moshoeshoe's ear. "It is a sign of power," he said. Also he gave Moshoeshoe an ox, a shield, and a spear. The boy asked Mohlomi to tell him what medicine gave him such power over men. Mohlomi answered, "Power is not gained by medicines ; the heart is the medicine."

Mohlomi and Moshoeshoe met again a few years later, when the eager lad had grown to noble manhood and was already a married man. The clear eyes of the sage saw the

change and promise which years had brought. " My son,"
he said, " if thou wouldst forsake all I would take thee with
me whithersoever I go, but it may not be. One day thou
shalt rule men. Learn then to know them. And when
thou judgest, let thy judgments be just."

It is told in the stories of Basutoland that the mark of
Mohlomi was seen on Moshoeshoe to the end of his life.

THE MAKING OF A NATION

Moshoeshoe was not born to the chieftainship of a great
tribe. His father ruled over a village and carried on its
affairs in the *lekhotla* or court. Local business was done
there, and strangers sometimes came and went. Moshoeshoe
spent long days watching and learning ; Mohlomi had told
him to get to know men. Presently people began to listen
whenever Moshoeshoe spoke. They were ready to gather
round him because he was wise and strong. First men
came one by one, then broken fragments of tribes sought his
shelter.

Moshoeshoe's ears must have been full of rumours of
what was happening beyond the mountains. The tribes of
South Africa were seething with unrest. Tshaka, the great
Zulu warrior chief, whose story has already been written,
was at the height of his power. His resistless armies left
ruin in their track. And further to the south, the white
settlers, Dutch and English, were slowly pushing northwards
towards the regions swept by the fighting tribes.

The man who could at such an hour begin to build a
nation had truly the gift of leadership. About the year
1820 Moshoeshoe moved to a village of his own. He chose
Butha-Buthe, where his wife's relations lived. The un-
settled wanderers who drifted to and fro belonged to many
tribes, spoke many dialects, and their habits and customs
were unlike. But they gathered one and all round Moshoeshoe, until these scattered groups, including even little
parties of Zulus, all owned him as chief. They chose to
follow his fortunes and he welded them into a new Basuto
nation, destined to play a great part in South African history.

Moshoeshoe would gladly have led the growing nation into ways of peace. But the times drove him to war. Here are four stories of fierce attacks made upon him.

1. The first great attack came from the Batlokoa, led by Sekonyela. They fell upon Butha-Buthe in force. Moshoeshoe drew back into his mountain fortress and was besieged. He saw his cattle captured as they went to water, his crops destroyed in the fields. Death drew nearer every day. A secret messenger found for him a better stronghold twenty miles to the south. But how could a besieged chief move his tribe, with women, children, old people, and cattle, through a country beset with foes?

Moshoeshoe heard that a band of fighting Zulus were not far off, looking for something to devour. So he sent a secret message to tell them that the Batlokoa were besieging Butha-Buthe and had great herds of cattle in their camp. The Zulus swooped down by night and routed Sekonyela in a fierce battle. He hastily raised the siege and withdrew. Then Moshoeshoe set off with his people to the new stronghold. The hill to which Moshoeshoe led his people was Thaba Bosiu, the Mountain of Night. There the Basuto chiefs have ruled and have been buried, Moshoeshoe, the great Chief of the Mountain, being the first.

2. By the year 1827 the Basuto had great wealth in cattle. The Amangwane wanted them and sent armies to carry off the herds. Moshoeshoe looked abroad at dawn one morning and there below him were the advancing hosts. In a moment Thaba Bosiu was called to arms. The Chief posted his sons Letsie and Molapo to guard the pass to the citadel, and himself led the attack. The Basuto were fighting for their existence. Though greatly outnumbered they put the enemy to flight. The Amangwane were so sure of success that girls had brought great jars of beer to celebrate their triumph. They fled, leaving the contents of their jars to refresh the victors. After this battle the power of Moshoeshoe was established and a national rejoicing was held.

3. The following year Moshoeshoe asked Sekonyela to supervise the initiation school for him in his absence.

Sekonyela took the opportunity of raiding Thaba Bosiu. While his soldiers were carrying off cattle, and also the Chief's principal wife and other women, they were attacked with fury by the Basuto and completely routed. When Moshoeshoe returned his anger rose high. But instead of seeking revenge for the treachery and insult he sent Sekonyela a present of cattle, and a rebuke which made him hang his head.

4. Not long after a Matabele army came to Thaba Bosiu in search of spoil. The Basuto were up early trying to strengthen their defences ; looking down they saw the dreaded Matabele on the banks of a little stream below, bathing, dancing, and arranging their war ornaments. Great piles of stones were made ready to be rained down on the enemies' heads. There was a fierce rush upward of the Matabele, a flight of assegais, and an avalanche of great stones from the Basuto above. Again the Matabele led their warriors against the rocky ramparts. Again they were forced back. Next morning the Matabele lost heart and began to return disconsolate to their chief. Suddenly a man from Moshoeshoe overtook them and spoke thus : " Moshoeshoe salutes you. Supposing that hunger has brought you to his country he sends you some cattle that you may eat them on your way home."

One of the Basutoland missionaries met some Matabele in Cape Town years later. He asked if they knew the Chief of the Basuto. They replied quickly, " Know him ? Yes ! That is the man who, having rolled down rocks on our heads, sent us oxen for food. We will never attack him again." And they kept their word.

The Coming of the Missionaries

Moshoeshoe was now between forty and fifty years of age. He longed for peace that he might build up the Basuto nation. He saw that new forces were moving in South Africa and that without education his people would be overwhelmed. Where could he find help ? Stories reached him of white missionaries living with tribes to the west and

south. He had once met two white hunters who were kind
when his people were starving. Yes—he would try to have
a missionary of his own. Some of his people objected ;
they did not want white men in their midst. But Moshoeshoe was never afraid to take risks for something worth
having. He would have a missionary if a missionary could
be found.

About this time a tall dark Griqua, Adam Krotz by
name, was hunting on the borders of Basutoland. He came
from Philippolis, near the Orange river. He was a member
of the Christian Church. Two Basuto met him and invited
him to come up and see the Chief. Moshoeshoe soon found
that there were missionaries in Philippolis and that the
people lived in peace. " Could you send me a missionary ? "
asked the Chief eagerly. Krotz was not sure, but he would
try. Moshoeshoe, afraid that his request might be forgotten,
sent a large herd of cattle after the hunter, with the message,
" Do not forget that Moshoeshoe wants a man of prayer."
The cattle were stolen by raiders. But Krotz remembered,
as we shall see.

Meantime, far away in France, three young men were
preparing to start for Africa. Two of them, Casalis and
Arbousset, were ministers, the third was an artisan. They
were going to join some French Protestant missionaries at
Mosiga, where the chief of the Bahurutu lived. But a
terrible disappointment awaited them at Cape Town. The
Matabele had swept down on Mosiga and dispersed the tribe.
The missionaries had gone up to the mission at Kuruman,
where a few years later David Livingstone came. Dr. Philip,
a missionary at Cape Town known for his great love for the
Natives, advised the young Frenchmen to go to Kuruman
too. But on the long journey they came to Philippolis,
called after their Cape Town friend. Here as mists roll off
a mountain side the cloud lifted from their future. For
Adam Krotz had returned from his hunting and soon the
three travellers were listening with wonder to his tale.
They would be " the men of prayer " whom the Chief of the
Mountain sought.

So they changed their course and set off for Basutoland

with Adam Krotz as their guide. As they reached the western borders of Basutoland it became easy to see why Moshoeshoe needed help. Human bones were strewn everywhere. Some places looked like battlefields. Tilled fields had lost their boundaries and gone wild again. Broken pots and fallen walls overgrown with briers showed where villages had been. The few inhabited houses were perched high on rocks for safety. Marks of desolation were all round. As they drew near Thaba Bosiu, the fields under the protection of the Chief were fair with crops and the people lived in safety.

At last the time to wait on the great Chief came. Leaving the wagons and the rest of the party to follow, young Casalis with Adam Krotz and his interpreter rode off. The mountain rose steeply before them. Its summit was dotted with the dark huts of the town. On the edge of the precipice a row of people stood watching their coming. They looked as small as crows. Casalis and Krotz first rode up a steep path, then, dismounting, they led their horses up rocky steps. As they set foot on the summit there was a rush to see the white man. Suddenly the crowd drew back and formed into a semicircle behind a man who advanced and seated himself upon a mat. " There is Moshoeshoe," said Adam Krotz. The great Chief and his man of prayer were face to face.

" The Chief," wrote Casalis afterwards, " bent upon me a look at once majestic and benevolent. His profile was much more aquiline than that of most of his subjects. His well-formed forehead, the fullness and regularity of his features, and his eyes—a little weary but full of intelligence and softness—made a deep impression on me. I felt at once that I had to do with a superior man, trained to think, to command others and, above all, to control himself."

The two men looked at each other in silence for a moment. Then Moshoeshoe rose. " Welcome, white man ! " he said. Casalis held out his hand. Then the Chief led his guest to the house where Mamahoto, his chief wife, lived. She sat on a mat before a fire in the palisaded courtyard. Casalis was soon enjoying a pot of milk and some bread.

How he used his eyes! He saw that Mamahoto was tall
and strong and attractive. She looked at him very kindly
as if she would like to mother him a little (he was only
twenty-one). He noticed that Moshoeshoe sat beside her,
with their youngest son, a boy of four or five, playing
between his knees. The Chief spoke to her with affection
and respect.

That was the first of many talks. As soon as the wagons
came the missionaries invited Moshoeshoe to dinner. They

MOSHOESHOE (*from an original drawing*).

had no plates. But they prepared a hash of mutton and
pumpkins. Moshoeshoe ate this off the lid of the saucepan
while the missionaries ate together out of the pot. Hot
coffee was served. The Chief hesitated over the colour, but
he found that with many handfuls of sugar coffee certainly
tasted good.

After dinner plans were made. The missionaries heard
about the Chief's anxieties. They promised to share the lot

of the Basuto and to teach them about God. They asked for some well-watered land where they could grow new crops of value to the people. Moshoeshoe found them a deep fertile valley about twenty miles from Thaba Bosiu, which the inhabitants had left. The missionaries settled there in July, 1833, and called their station Moriah (Morija). Thus began a friendship between the Basuto people and their missionaries which has lasted ever since. To-day the French Protestant Mission is actively at work, and has built up a living Christian Church with Basuto leaders and many schools. There are also missions of the Church of England and the Roman Catholics. Many have followed in the footsteps of Moshoeshoe's first " man of prayer."

A Chief at Work

In Basutoland, as elsewhere in Africa, a good chief is a busy man. Moshoeshoe often asked the missionaries to come to see him in the middle of the night, for he had no free time by day. The chief was related to the whole life of the tribe. He held the land in trust and gave the use of it to the cultivators. He had the right to claim certain labour from the people and to impose certain taxes. All national and religious ceremonies were under his direction. He had to taste the first fruits before the harvest could be gathered in. He was the head and centre of the tribal organisation for the administration of justice and the making of laws.

The *pitso* or National Council of Basutoland, which met to deal with such questions as change of law or decisions as to going to war, was summoned by the chief. No man whom he called could refuse to come. This old Basuto parliament exists in a modified form to-day. In 1903 large and clearly defined responsibility was given to it.[1]

Each little clan or village chieftain had his *lekhotla*, or court, where local work was done. But the *lekhotla* of a great chief like Moshoeshoe was a centre of wide administrative work. Day by day he spent long hours in this focus

---

[1] For an instance of its modern working, see p. 114.

of tribal life, often eating his meals there, so that even the poorest man could have access to him at any time. The chief sat in the middle with his headmen and counsellors on either side. Cases were argued at great length. Many witnesses were heard. The proceedings were dignified. No noise was allowed, except when some clever answer drew applause from the crowd of spectators. At the close of a case the counsellor of lowest rank spoke first. The others gave their opinion in proper order. Last of all spoke the chief and his decision was final.

Though Moshoeshoe was an unlettered man, his ability, foresight, and courage made him easily a leader among the tribes. But the days in which he lived brought him into touch with white men. He had to decide questions which earlier chiefs had never faced. The boundaries of his territory had to be defended and defined. Raiders, not Natives only, but half-castes and even unworthy white men, had to be repulsed. His sons and younger chieftains fell into wild ways and had to be restrained.

All the time Moshoeshoe was working to improve the condition of his people and to make wise laws. He sent three of his sons to Cape Town to be educated and learn white men's ways. He valued what the missionaries did to uplift the Basuto. Though he never joined the Christian Church during his years of activity, he gave its work support and its teachings influenced his life. He encouraged schools. Among the laws he made was one to check the liquor traffic. He never drank brandy himself. White men were welcome to open shops for trade in Basutoland, but Moshoeshoe always reserved for the Basuto the land on which the shops were built.

The great Chief of the Mountain was a just judge and an able law-giver. He had known how to turn many enemies into friends. He held the love and confidence of his people. He led them safely through many perils. He sought nothing for himself and never worked for private ends. He faced with rare courage and prudence situations before which any man might have quailed. One white official after another bore witness to his high character and his power of handling

affairs. In matters touching his own tribe he often showed
shrewd humour and wisdom beyond that of most men.
Here is an instance of this.

In the days when the people were homeless and starving,
cannibalism became common among some of the tribes.
In sheer misery hungry wretches began to eat their fellows.
The dreadful taste grew, even among some of the Basuto.
Moshoeshoe was wise enough to know that want rather than
wickedness was the cause. As chief he might have punished
the evil doers ; instead he gave them food and cattle and
encouraged them to plant crops.

When Moshoeshoe was moving from Butha-Buthe to
Thaba Bosiu (see p. 17), his grandfather Peete got left
behind on the hasty journey. The cannibals caught him
and ate him up. Some years after, Moshoeshoe's eldest
son, Letsie, was ready to go to the initiation school, but could
not be admitted till his ancestors' graves had been purified.
But as his great-grandfather had been eaten by cannibals,
there was a break in the generations. How could it be
bridged ? The group of cannibals who had eaten the old
man were known. Moshoeshoe was urged to have them put
to death. But he never killed a man if he could avoid it.
With dry humour he said, " It is not becoming to disturb the
graves of your ancestors." Then he gave orders that the
cannibals and their chief should be purified as if they really
were the old ancestor's grave. The way was then clear for
Letsie to go to the school.

TROUBLOUS DAYS

Moshoeshoe had no fear or distrust of white men. More
perhaps than any other African he had a genius for dealing
with them and understanding their ways. He was able in
difficult days to draw up letters full of point and wisdom
setting tangled situations before officials. The missionaries
wrote down these letters for him, but no one can doubt that
they are the fruit of a far-seeing African mind.

Moshoeshoe could always work with a group of white
men for common ends. But when in territories round

Basutoland there were two white races who had not yet come to good terms with one another, and even fought at times, life was anxious for the Mountain Chief. Then, too, for an unlettered man, however able, treaties and agreements, boundaries and maps, were puzzling things. In conference Moshoeshoe could meet any one. But when one white governor agreed to do what he wanted, and then a new one came and changed what had been planned, the Chief felt wronged. There were so many white authorities to deal with, and they came and went. The Orange River territory on one side and the Transvaal on the other were sometimes under Dutch sometimes under British rule. Basutoland itself was at one time entirely independent. Then it was made a treaty state under British sovereignty. Then it was left independent again, with no fixed boundary between it and the Orange Free State Republic belonging to the Boers. Between 1851 and 1867 Moshoeshoe was four times at war with the Dutch and once with the British.

The times were as puzzling for the white men as they were for him. Both sides made mistakes. As Moshoeshoe grew older, men said that he was sometimes not straightforward. It may be so. But few men, white or black, have faced such odds and borne such heavy burdens and kept their hands so clean. When the Chief saw he had done wrong he was not ashamed to admit it. He once wrote to the Governor of the Cape : " My people became restless and took some advantage of their angry feelings to carry off cattle and horses. This I did not approve."

One of Moshoeshoe's letters, written after the battle of Berea, has become quite famous. The Basuto had been plundering and raiding with persistency and success. The Dutch farmers could bear it no longer and complained to the British at the Cape. In December, 1852, the Governor marched northward, bringing a strong force to overawe the Basuto. He made careful inquiries on the spot. There was evidence that the Basuto were in the wrong. He said they must return the cattle they had stolen and pay a heavy fine. So the demand was made for 10,000 head of horned cattle and 1,000 horses, to be delivered within three days.

The Basuto were not at all prepared to obey this order. In any case they could not collect and deliver so large a number in so short a time. Moshoeshoe sent 3,500 head of cattle, saying he could do no better. Then he withdrew into his mountain fastness to see what would come to pass.

The Governor was not anxious for battle, but order had to be maintained. His forces advanced in three divisions upon Thaba Bosiu. The first was drawn into an ambush and was forced to retreat, having captured great herds of cattle. The second division was repulsed in an attack and had to camp among the rocks, where the third division joined it. In the morning the General decided to withdraw to his former camp. His forces marched back through the open country. A great body of armed Basuto kept pace with them by marching along the ridge of Berea mountain which flanked the plain. It was a triumph for Moshoeshoe. But he cared for no victory that did not lead to peace.

In the quiet of the night time, while the attacking armies slept, he called one of his missionaries to write a letter to the Governor. It was dispatched in the morning after the retreating forces by a somewhat reluctant messenger. As the British drew near their camp on the Caledon, the Basuto envoy overtook them and bore to the Governor the message the Chief sent. These were its words :—

Thaba Bosiu.
Midnight, December 20th, 1852.

YOUR EXCELLENCY,

This day you have fought against my people and taken much cattle. As the object for which you have come is to have a compensation for the Boers, I beg you will be satisfied with what you have taken. I entreat peace from you. You have chastised, let it be enough, I pray you ; and let me be no longer considered an enemy to the Queen. I will try all I can to keep my people in order for the future.

Your humble servant,
MOSHOESHOE.

The letter was accepted. The British army marched away.

The heavy strain of a hard life had left its mark upon Moshoeshoe. With resource and ability he urged his desire that Basutoland might come under the direct control of the British Imperial Government. He had a passionate belief in the justice and protective power of the Queen. The years of his old age were long and weary. Eight or ten years before he died he said to his people : " You must listen that you may know what I have done for you when I was young and strong. Now I am old, and about to become blind like an old goat." His bodily strength was exhausted, his clear mind dimmed. He was no longer consulted or honoured. His sons controlled his followers without reference to him. He watched and watched for news of the future of his country. Four months before his death he chose a beautiful kaross of panther skins to be sent to Queen Victoria. At last, the news came that his wish was granted, Basutoland was to be under direct British control. On March 11th, 1870, Moshoeshoe died, aged over seventy years.

He had passed so long from active life that the colonial papers scarcely noticed that the greatest African was gone. But for the Basuto death transformed the old man they had almost forgotten into a hero and the Great Chief of the Mountain lived again. Memories of what he had been to them and done for them quickened. Thaba Bosiu became not only the fortress which had never been taken, but the sacred place where the body of Moshoeshoe lay in their midst.

LIVINGSTONE'S AFRICAN FRIENDS

I. TO AND FRO IN AFRICA

OUR first concern is not with Livingstone but with his African friends. He is like the background of a picture against which the figures in the foreground stand out. He is like the centre round which many men circle and in relation to which they move. We are going to think of Africans as the great explorer knew them. But to find his friends we must follow his journeys and share his fortunes in camp and on the road.

The Man and his Journeys

The story of David Livingstone, the Scottish boy of ancient lineage who wanted to be a missionary, is known to all the world. He learned Greek and Latin while working fourteen hours a day in a cotton mill near Glasgow. He qualified as a doctor of medicine. He arrived in South Africa as a medical missionary in July, 1841, being then twenty-eight years of age.

David Livingstone went first to Kuruman, where the Moffats welcomed him in their missionary home. In due time, under an almond tree in the garden, he won their daughter, Mary Moffat, to be his wife. Together they set up house at Mabotsa, 200 miles to the north-east. Two years later they moved further north to the Bakwena people, where Sechele (see p. 35) was chief. They made their home on the Kolobeng river for a time. Children were born to them and the home was full of love. From the first Livingstone pushed out into the unknown. He explored the Kalahari desert ; he discovered Lake Ngami,

28

he even took his family far northward to where Sebituane (see p. 39) was ruling the great Makololo tribe. Then his wife's health broke down. Livingstone took her to Cape Town, whence she went to England. She only returned to Africa to die.

Livingstone's three main journeys are shown on the map on p. 30. The lines are like a great cross laid on the southern half of Africa.

The Way of the Cross

First Journey.—From Cape Town, after parting with his wife, Livingstone returned to Linyanti. Sekeletu (see p: 42) was the reigning chief. No suitable site for a home could be found. The country was languishing for an outlet for healthy trade. Slaves were becoming the main merchandise. No one could tell whether the Makololo, who were in the centre of Africa, could trade best to the west or the east. Livingstone resolved to explore in both directions, first westward to the Atlantic Ocean, then to the Indian Ocean on the east. A few sentences can record this adventurous journey through unknown lands, but it cost Livingstone two and a half years of strenuous toil.

By the time he and his Makololo followers had reached S. Paul de Loanda on the Atlantic it was clear that trade would not be opened with the west. Retracing their toilsome way to Linyanti they halted for a little and started towards the east. The glorious Victoria Falls on the Zambezi were passed—one of the wonders of the world. On, on, through lands unknown to any white man went Livingstone and his band. But still their search was vain. The only trade was in human flesh. The horror of the slave trade grew. First Tete and then Quilimane on the Indian Ocean were reached. Thence the traveller, who had been in Africa for nearly sixteen years, went home in 1856. He promised that if his Makololo followers waited in Tete till his return he would take them back to their homes. This promise, though at great cost to himself, he loyally fulfilled. Livingstone had a noble welcome in England, for the fame of his journey rang through the world. To be once more with his wife and children refreshed his lonely heart.

Second Journey.—Little more than a year later Africa called him again. Though in heart and life he remained a Christian missionary, he went back as a British Consul with

headquarters at Quilimane. He was to lead an expedition
to explore East and Central Africa. He reached Zanzibar
in March, 1858. The next six years brought broken work

THE JOURNEYS OF DAVID LIVINGSTONE.

and heavy disappointment. Progress was made in exploring
the rivers Rovuma, Shire, and Zambezi, and Lakes Shirwa and
Nyasa. The misery and cruelty of the slave trade haunted him.
The steam launch on which hopes had been built proved worth-

less. The Universities' Mission, which Livingstone had been eager to see at work on the Shire river, lost its first bishop and transferred its headquarters to the island of Zanzibar.

In the year 1862 there fell the dark shadow of Mary Livingstone's death. She had longed intensely to rejoin her husband in Africa. In January, 1862, she came. Four months later she fell ill in lovely Shupanga, near the entrance to the Zambezi river. In a week she was dead, and they laid her to rest under a great baobab tree. Finally funds ran short in England, and the Expedition was recalled. Livingstone himself navigated a little steamer he had been using on the African rivers right across the Indian Ocean to Bombay. There he left the boat, and two of his African helpers, and went home to England once more.

Third Journey.—A year later Livingstone set out for Africa again. Two ideas burned within him. One was that slavery could only be checked by opening up Africa to honest trade, the other that the river Nile had its true source in fountains in the Zambezi-Congo watershed, not in the Victoria Nyanza as Speke and Grant had declared. He thought the Lualaba might be the Nile. In this Livingstone was mistaken. But a passionate desire to find the southernmost source of the Nile dominated the rest of his life.

Picking up his boat and his helpers at Bombay, Livingstone reached Zanzibar in January, 1866. Two months later he was on the Rovuma river. His journey can be followed on the map. The line goes to and fro, round to the south of Lake Nyasa, northwards to Lake Tanganyika, then to Lake Bangweolo, discovered in 1868. In the long drawn-out records of that journey the pace seems to get slower, the fever more persistent, the difficulties greater, the slave raiders more daring. By March, 1869, Livingstone, scarcely able to keep going, was back at Ujiji on Lake Tanganyika. Thence he made a disastrous attempt to reach and explore the Lualaba river, now known as an affluent of the Congo; he still hoped it might prove to be the Nile. Sick at heart, the weary traveller turned westward and crossed the lake to Ujiji. Never had his hopes been so low.

Five days later, on October 18th, 1871, Henry Stanley, sent by the owner of a well known New York newspaper, walked into the little camp. New hope came to the ailing man. Good news from home, good food for his famished body, changed the aspect of things. Stanley gave him the reverent honour which a young man feels for a great man nearing the end of his career. Together

they explored the north end of the lake and went on to Unyanyembe. Then with mutual love they parted, for no persuasions
would bring Livingstone home. Once more, for just another
year, he must seek to know the unknown. Stanley pushed his
way back to the coast to give the waiting world news of Livingstone. In five months the supplies he sent up from the coast
reached Livingstone's camp. Then the explorer for the last time
set his face towards the spongy jungles round Lake Bangweolo.
Eight months later, on May 1st, 1873, Livingstone died at
Chitambo's village in Ilala.

Travelling Acquaintances and Helpers

When a man is always travelling he makes many
acquaintances but few friends. Livingstone got into really
close touch with Sechele, Sebituane (though they were only
a short time together), and Sekeletu. But in his thirty
years of travel he made acquaintance with hundreds of
chiefs. Insight and imagination enabled him to measure
the worth of men. The charm of his manner, the courtesy
of his bearing, the pains he took to remove distrust com-
mended him to those he met. Africans love humour of the
kind which Livingstone displayed. His sturdy refusal to be
played upon never gave offence. In a word, he was a MAN.
MEN generally understand one another, even if one is black
and the other white.

Livingstone's journals are full of little word pictures of
chiefs. Sometimes on the outward journey a chief would
be suspicious ; on the return journey he was generally ready
to be a friend. Now and then in a few vivid phrases a
woman chief, full of character and determination—and
sometimes of kindness—is sketched. To many chiefs
Livingstone was an object of curiosity as the first white man
they had seen. Others feared him, believing he was in
league with slave-hunting Arabs or Portuguese. Some
looked on him with greed, coveting what he possessed. But
Livingstone was not rich like other travellers. His resources
were always small. He paid out cattle, cloth, and beads in
fair exchange for value given. He gave presents too, when
he could. But supplies often failed him and he could neither

buy nor make gifts. Many chiefs who gave him food when he and his men were hungry got nothing in return. Again and again generous hospitality was shown to the white traveller in distress. Instances of African courtesy were often as graceful as that for which Livingstone was renowned.

Some chiefs were arrogant and treacherous and drunken. Livingstone's keen eye saw it all. His love for Africans was not based on blindness to their faults. His soul was sometimes sickened by what he saw. Guns and ammunition he was often asked for. But as the use to be made of them was quite uncertain he withheld them whenever he could. His wrath rose when a chief asked him for a man to be sold as a slave. "I would rather die than give him a man," he wrote after one such request. It would be interesting to know what all these chiefs, both good and bad, thought of the white man who came, stayed a night or two, and then passed on. They must have talked him over in tribal councils and wondered at some of his ways. But written records were not kept in his day by tribes in Central Africa. We only know two things. One is that later travellers found Livingstone's name held in living remembrance in places through which he had passed. The other is that Arab slave-traders followed on the tracks that he had opened. They used his name and sought to profit by the confidence he had won.

African travellers depend for comfort, sometimes even for life itself, upon the men who arrange the details of their journeys and those who carry the loads. There are splendid stories of courage, endurance, and faithfulness. There are also stories of desertion and dishonesty on the one hand, of harshness, anger, and injustice on the other. Sometimes there is constant strife between the master and the men. To Livingstone attendants and carriers were fellow-men to be considered and cared for. He won their affection and returned their loyalty by gentleness, kindness, and grateful remembrance of their good deeds. One of the greatest stories in the world is the devotion of the attendants who were with him when he died. But even to him helpers were not always faithful. One of his men deserted, appeared at

Zanzibar, and told a long story of Livingstone's death. Before the falsehood was discovered a search expedition had been sent out to Africa.

Quite early in the Kuruman days a young attendant named Sehamy died. Livingstone's journal is full of lament. He recalls the loving service of the lad. He went to comfort him when he was taken ill. Another journeying friend was Mebalwe, a young Christian schoolmaster from Kuruman who travelled with Livingstone for a time. He is the hero of the lion story at Mabotsa. Livingstone had wounded a lion, one of a group which had been ravaging a Bakwena village. While he was re-loading his rifle, the lion sprang upon him, seized him by the arm and shoulder, shook him as a terrier shakes a rat, and stood over him growling horribly. Mebalwe, only ten or fifteen yards away, bravely tried to shoot, but both barrels of his flint gun missed fire. The lion sprang from Livingstone, seized Mebalwe and bit him in the thigh. Another man, whose life Livingstone had saved when a buffalo tossed him, tried to drive the lion off with a spear. But suddenly Livingstone's first bullets did their work and the lion fell down dead. Mebalwe's courage saved Livingstone's life. To the end his arm showed the marks of the lion's teeth. The crushed bone never regained shape, the joint was always weak.

It is interesting to see how largely Mebalwe figures in after days. He helps to build a house for Livingstone. Livingstone plans a house for him. Mebalwe teaches the alphabet. He travels with Livingstone up to Sebituane's. He is offered work close to a threatening neighbour who proposes to kill him. Livingstone refuses to let him take the post. When Kolobeng was attacked (see p. 38) the commando first drove off all Mebalwe's cattle and then went to hear him preach in church. Finally, in 1854, more than eleven years after Mebalwe began to help Livingstone, the explorer, on his way from Linyanti to Loanda, wrote to tell his wife of the excellence of the Makalolo who were travelling with him. " They are the best set of men I ever travelled with," he said, " except Mebalwe."

There were not in Livingstone's day many Africans who

had won for themselves professional qualifications or taken responsible part with white men in public work. Later on we shall find the life story of some of these. Mebalwe's education was slender. Sechele learned the alphabet long after he was a chief. Some of Livingstone's attendants became expert in helping him in his scientific observations and in making maps. For the rest few of his African friends could read or write. Yet he discerned their qualities and had no doubt of their capacity for serving mankind. " I have no fears," he once said in England, " as to the mental and moral capacity of the Africans for civilisation and upward progress. . . . I who have been intimate with Africans . . . believe them to be capable of holding an honourable rank in the family of man."

II. SECHELE, CHIEF OF THE BAKWENA

An Apt Pupil

Mochoasele, chief of the Bakwena, had worn out the patience of the tribe by his bad character and dissolute life. So his subjects put him to death. There was disagreement as to his successor. One party wanted a distant relative of Mochoasele as their permanent chief. Another party wanted young Sechele, Mochoasele's son. The first party got their man into office. The second party appealed to Sebituane, chief of the Makololo, who was in the neighbourhood on his great northward march just then. It was the sort of invitation which appealed to an African chief. The Makololo came by night and surrounded the kraal of the Bakwena.

At early dawn a Makololo herald proclaimed that Sebituane had come to avenge the murder of Mochoasele. All the warriors beat loudly upon their shields. The panic-stricken Bakwena, roused from slumber, rushed wildly to and fro. The Makololo speared them as they tried to escape. Sechele, who was in the kraal, was as much alarmed as the rest. But Sebituane had given orders that the boy was to be taken care of. So a Makololo warrior stunned him by a blow on the head and rolled the unconscious lad out of the way till the fight was over. The usurper was killed. Sechele was made chief. The Makololo, unlike their usual custom, went away without taking any plunder for themselves.

Sechele was well-established as ruler of his people when Livingstone settled among the Bakwena in 1845. The two men were attracted to each other at once. A friendship quickly sprang up between them. Sechele was tall and spare, with large eyes. Being very dark his people called him " Black Sechele." He was a man of vigorous and independent spirit. Men who compared him with other great chiefs said he was second in ability only to Moshoeshoe. He was as loving and original as Khama, but not so strong a character.

At the first Christian service held by Livingstone Sechele announced that the Bakwena liked to ask questions when they heard new things. The Chief set himself to learn reading and an apt pupil he was. He was so eager to get on quickly that he gave up hunting and sat at his studies for hours. Soon he could read quite well. Livingstone had often to pass by the Chief's house, and Sechele loved to call him in that he might read the Bible aloud. He liked the Book of Isaiah the prophet best. " He was a fine man, that Isaiah," said Sechele. " He knew how to speak."

The Chief and the missionary both wanted the Bakwena to become Christians. But Sechele was puzzled by Livingstone's gentle ways. " Do you imagine these people will ever believe by your merely talking to them ? " he asked. " I can make them do nothing except' by thrashing them. If you like, I will call my head men and with our whips of rhinoceros hide we will soon make them all believe together." The idea of persuading or winning his subjects was new to him. Later on he understood that when it comes to religion a chief cannot change men's hearts. " In former times," he said, " when a chief was fond of hunting, all his people got dogs and became fond of hunting too. If he was fond of dancing or music, so were they. If the chief loved beer, they all rejoiced in strong drink. But in this case it is different. I love the word of God and not one of my people will join me."

For more than two years Sechele lived as a Christian in
full view of his people, walking uprightly in all relations of
life. Then he asked that he might be baptised. This
raised a question which has often perplexed true and honest
men in Africa. For Sechele had many wives. He felt it
was hard to put them away from him. Livingstone, who
knew these wives and had often taught them, could understand what it cost. He did not tell Sechele what to do ; he
only said, " You can read the Bible for yourself." Sechele
read that in old days good men like Abraham sometimes had
more than one wife, but he read, too, that the teaching of
Jesus was against the old way. To be a Christian he must
have only one wife. He often said to Livingstone, " I wish
you had come to this country before I was entangled in the
meshes of its customs." But the Chief had made up his
mind. He gave all his wives, except the first one, new
clothes and all the goods in their huts. He sent them back
to their parents, saying he found no fault with them, but
that he himself had to follow the will of God. Then he and
his children were baptised.

By the Kolobeng River—and After

Sechele had no easy time. The relatives of the wives he
had sent home became his bitter enemies. A severe drought
began and lasted for four years. Now Sechele had been a
noted rain doctor and found it more difficult to give up
rain-making than anything else. The Bakwena believed
that Livingstone had bound Sechele with a magic spell so
that he might not make rain for them. They thought that
the presence of the missionary caused the lack of rain.
Deputations of the old counsellors came to him. " Let the
Chief make only a few showers," they said. " The corn will
die if you refuse and we shall become scattered. Only let
him make rain this once and we shall all, men, women, and
children, come to the school and sing and pray as long as you
please."

One of Sechele's uncles, a sensible person of wide influence, came to Livingstone one day. " We like you," he

said, " as if you had been born among us. You are the only
white man we can become familiar with. But we wish you
to give up preaching and praying ; we cannot be familiar with
that at all. We never get rain, and those tribes who never
pray get it in abundance." Livingstone at last persuaded
the people that in a land so dry they must make their home
near a never-failing river. He himself, he told them, was
going to live on the banks of the Kolobeng river, some forty
miles away. There he could teach them how to make a
canal and irrigate their land. So Livingstone trekked with
all his belongings. The next morning the whole tribe began
to move too.

At the new town beside the Kolobeng river the Chief and
the missionaries worked in happy fellowship until there
broke upon them one of those times of trouble which arise
in half-settled lands. Between Sechele and the emigrant
farmers in the Transvaal misunderstandings had arisen.
Each thought the other wholly in the wrong. It is a
tangled story, and we cannot unravel it here. Livingstone
had gone to Cape Town whence his wife and children were
starting for England. On his way back to Kolobeng a
heartbroken letter was brought to him from Sechele's wife
to say a commando had attacked Kolobeng, killed many
people, carried off children, burned the corn, and swept
away the cattle. On arrival at Kolobeng Livingstone found
his own house—the only real home he ever possessed in
Africa—pillaged and ruined, its simple treasures scattered
or destroyed.

There are two stories as to the authors of this wanton
destruction. It is not our duty to judge between them or
to apportion blame. The deed was done. It convinced
Livingstone that the emigrant farmers were strongly opposed
to his work. This made him more resolved than ever to
press on into the furthest heart of Africa with the message
he had to give. He therefore passed on northward to the
Makololo and beyond them. He worked in Kolobeng no
more. Sechele took his wife and children to the kindly
Moffats at Kuruman, and went himself to the Cape to see if
reparation could be had. He wanted the Queen of England

to intervene on his behalf. That could not be ; but at the Cape he met with kindness and was comforted.

Sechele moved his impoverished people from Kolobeng to a tract of dry and barely habitable country between the Transvaal and the Kalahari Desert. Here he thought they would be safe. Remnants of other tribes gathered round him and his people. They went through great privations, but prosperity came at last. Some years later Molepololo was built to be the capital of the Bakwena. When John Moffat, son of Robert Moffat at Kuruman, went to be Sechele's missionary he found the memory of Livingstone fresh and green. Heathen rites and ceremonies did not prevail in Molepololo. Sechele was still anxious that his people should be taught the Christian way of life. Though in some ways he was wayward and inconsistent, the Chief bore the marks of his friendship with David Livingstone to the end of his life. He played a large part in tribal politics in Khama's day, as we shall see, and on the whole his influence was for good.

III. SEBITUANE, CHIEF OF THE MAKOLOLO

Sebituane, builder of the Makololo nation, is one of the most striking figures in African tribal history. He only came for a short period into Livingstone's life, but the two men at once found one another and made friends.

Sebituane's mother was related to Mohlomi. He was the son of Mongoane, chieftain of a branch of the Bakofeng tribe which had settled on the Kurutlete mountains near the Vet river. The settlement was broken up in 1822 by an attack from the Mantatis. Roaming about in the confusion of the time the tribe gradually drew together. Mongoane died, and his eldest son was eaten by lions. Sebituane, then about nineteen years of age and married, became chief. He had already proved his valour.

When he proposed that the people who gathered round him should leave the land where they had been ruined by war they agreed. When he pointed to the north, whence legend said their forefathers had come, they were ready to follow. So the host of men, women, children and cattle set out on their amazing trek from the Vaal to the Zambezi river. Right through the heart of southern Africa, the Makololo, as Sebituane's people came to be called, fought their way. One tribe after another barred their advance. But the foes were defeated and the Makololo marched on. They turned now to the right, now to the left, but always moved forward. They followed their foes across rivers and ensnared them on islands in the stream. Many treacherous deeds stain the record of their progress. But Sebituane was far nobler than the tyrant Tshaka and had no lust for cruelty, no joy in taking life.

When he and his people finally came to rest in the neighbourhood of the Zambezi river west of the Victoria Falls, their fame as warriors was established throughout Central Africa. No wonder that the fearless Makololo, led by the greatest potentate of Central Africa, drew out Livingstone's desire. He and Sebituane were men who could stand up to one another. Three times Livingstone sought to reach the Chief. When he was forced the second time to retrace his steps, Sebituane sent thirteen brown cows to one chief, and thirteen red cows to another, and thirteen black cows to Sechele—whose life he had saved as a boy—asking each to help the white men to reach him.

At last, after a long and toilsome journey, Livingstone and his family really arrived. Sebituane had gone down the river to meet him. Livingstone followed in a canoe. They found Sebituane on an island with his principal men round him, all singing together. The Chief signified his joy, gave Livingstone an ox and a jar of honey, and skins of oxen, soft as cloth, to cover him at night. Then long before day Sebituane came and sat by Livingstone's fire under the hedge where he lay, and the two great men talked.

Sebituane was then about forty-five years of age, tall and wiry, of olive complexion and slightly bald. Livingstone was impressed by his frankness and his cool and collected manner. He was as remarkable in peace as he had been in war. He had the art of gaining the affection and confidence of men. Poor men who came to his town to sell the skins of animals they had killed were welcomed. The Chief would go to see them himself and order attendants to bring them meal and milk and honey that they might feast. He never allowed a party of strangers to leave without presenting gifts to them and even to their servants.

As a result of this benevolence, the praises of Sebituane sounded far and near. " He has a heart! He is wise! He knows how to rule! " his people said of him. Because he was so frank and open with them they talked freely to him. He was aware of all that was happening in the country. He was greatly pleased that Livingstone had brought his children with him. It was a mark of confidence, he felt. He was willing that the white man should settle as a missionary among the Makololo. He would take Livingstone through all their country to choose the right place to begin his work.

Then just as he began to know the white man for whose coming he had waited, Sebitaune was seized with an acute illness from which he had suffered before. Within a few days he died. It was a great blow to Livingstone's hopes and a loss for Central Africa.

" I visited him in company with my little boy Robert on the Sunday afternoon on which he died," wrote Livingstone. " ' Come near,' said Sebituane, ' and see if I am any longer a man ; I am done.' I ventured to assent and added a single sentence about hope after death. ' Why do you speak of death ? ' said one of a relay of fresh doctors, ' Sebituane will never die.' After sitting with him for some time, and commending him to the mercy of God, I rose to depart. He raised himself up a little, called a servant, and said, ' Take Robert to Maunku (one of his wives) and tell her to give him some milk.' Those were the last words of Sebituane. . . . He was decidedly the best specimen of a Native chief that I have ever met. I was never so much grieved at the loss of a black man before."

IV. SEKELETU, SEBITUANE'S SON

Sebituane had arranged long beforehand that Mamochisane, daughter of his principal wife, should succeed him
as chief. She was a competent woman who had exercised
a good deal of local authority ; she was trained to rule. But
she had no taste for public life. She grew tired of responsibility and of the intrigues of court. She wanted to be a
woman, not a chief, and to live her own life. So she abdicated
in favour of her young half-brother Sekeletu, then eighteen
years of age. He shrank as much as she did from so onerous
a task. He offered to stand by her, if she would be chief.
But Mamochisane had made up her mind. A great meeting
of the people was called and lasted three days. But Mamochisane firmly declined to withdraw her decision and retired
to her local rule. Sekeletu became chief.

Livingstone had taken his family south to Cape Town
immediately after Sebituane's death. Before he returned to
the Makololo he had passed through the bitter experience
of the ruin of his home at Kolobeng.

Sekeletu's estimate of himself was unhappily right. He
was not a strong man like his father. He could not quite
rule his people or himself. Chieftainship does not make a
man ; it is the man that makes the chief. Sekeletu turned
for help to Livingstone. He called him his new father. He
begged him to settle in the tribe. He travelled with him
through the country seeking a healthy site for a mission
station. But none could be found. On this journey
Livingstone saved Sekeletu's life by stepping between him
and an assassin. On a later journey Sekeletu did a gracious
and a kindly act. He and Livingstone got separated from
their party in a forest on a dark and rainy night. The
luggage had all gone on. They had to sleep under a tree,
and Livingstone had no blanket. The young Chief insisted
on putting his own blanket over Livingstone and lay on the
wet ground himself.

Even in Sebituane's day the slave-trade had penetrated
among the Makololo. Some half-breed Portuguese appeared

with eight guns for sale. They would only exchange them for men. Sebituane reluctantly gave eight men for the guns. Next year the half-breeds offered to help in a warlike expedition. The Makololo could keep all the captured cattle if the prisoners were theirs. Before long the Makololo had bought three guns from some Arabs for thirty small boys. What was bad enough under a strong chief grew worse under the weak and inexperienced rule of Sekeletu. The people were very poor. The country was full of ivory for sale. Traders would buy nothing but men.

Livingstone knew that if a way to the coast could be found for Sekeletu's ivory the traffic in human beings could be stopped. In search of this he embarked on his first great journey westward from Linyanti to Loanda on the coast. Hopefully the traveller sought, through untraversed country and primeval forest, some way which human porterage could use. The quest was vain. Inquiries in Loanda brought no light. Back to Sekeletu, still hopeful, Livingstone made his way. Africa had another side. He would explore to the east.

Sekeletu welcomed Livingstone and liked the presents he had brought from the people in Loando. The treasured journals, the wagons, and the goods left behind by Livingstone had been kept safely and were faithfully yielded up. But Sekeletu had been going on marauding expeditions and his "new father" had to take him to task. Hopefully again Livingstone set off eastward. Sekeletu went with him to the Victoria Falls. As far as his influence reached he opened the traveller's way. But no facilities for trade, except in slaves, were found between Linyanti and the eastern coast.

From Quilimane Livingstone went to England. While the world honoured him for his adventurous journey he did not forget the young African Chief whose sore need had nerved him for the task. When Livingstone returned to the Makololo in the year 1860, he brought with him a letter addressed to " Our esteemed friend Sekeletu, Chief of the Makololo, South Central Africa." It was written by Lord Clarendon, the British Secretary of State for Foreign Affairs. It begins :

The Queen our Sovereign and the British Government have learnt with much pleasure from her Majesty's servant, Dr. Livingstone, the kind manner in which you co-operated with him in his endeavours to find a path from your country to the sea on the west coast, and again when he was following the course of the river Zambezi from your town to the eastern coast. You helped by furnishing him on each occasion with canoes, provisions, oxen, and men, free of expense.

The letter goes on to point out that the English are friends and promoters of all lawful commerce, but are the enemies of the slave trade and slave hunting.

Things were not going well with the Makololo. Some missionaries had been sent at Livingstone's request, but they died under circumstances which made some people fear they had been poisoned. There was severe drought in the land. Sebituane's great empire was beginning to break up. Livingstone was distressed for his friend. Sekeletu had developed leprosy and grown suspicious of his leading men. He thought himself bewitched. As always, he was kind to Livingstone and sent him a fine fat ox as a present. He shut himself away from his people. Strange rumours about him were going round. He sent, however, for Livingstone, who found him in a covered wagon enclosed by a high wall of close-set reeds. His face was only slightly disfigured. "He has," wrote Livingstone, "the quiet, unassuming manners of his father Sebituane, speaks distinctly in a low pleasant voice, and appears to be a sensible man, except, perhaps, on the subject of his having been bewitched."

The Native doctors had given up Sekeletu's case. They could not cure him. His last hope hung on an old doctress of the Manyeti tribe who was attempting his cure. It was characteristic of Livingstone's courtesy that he declined to take the case out of her hands. He was a doctor himself. " It is bad value to appear to undervalue any of the profession," he said. But the old doctress was induced to suspend her treatment for a month while Livingstone got to work. Sekeletu's health improved greatly. He became cheerful again. Though it was a time of great scarcity he regaled his guests with dainties. He gave them tea and excellent American biscuits, and preserved fruits which had been brought to him all the way from Benguella. But he resolutely refused to appear in public till he was perfectly cured and had regained his looks.

When Livingstone left the Makololo and returned to the east coast again, he took two tribesmen with him to bring back medicine for the Chief. But in 1864, when Livingstone was at Newstead Abbey in England (see pp. 48, 49), writing the story of his expedition to the Zambezi, news reached him that his poor friend Sekeletu had died.

V. THE LAST LONG MARCH

NOT SERVANTS BUT FRIENDS

When Stanley found Livingstone, five of his followers were well-known and trusted friends. Here are their names : Susi, a Shupanga man, had begun to serve Livingstone even before the death of his wife. He was first a wood-cutter for the little Zambezi steamer, the *Pioneer*, then he became the headman of Livingstone's party. Chuma was a Wayao. Livingstone and Bishop Mackenzie had rescued him from slavery in 1861. He spent three years in the mission before he became Livingstone's servant. He took the adventurous voyage to Bombay when Livingstone navigated the little *Lady Nyassa* across the Indian Ocean and remained there until Livingstone picked him up on his return journey from England. Amoda was also a Shupanga man and, like Susi, had been a wood-cutter for the *Pioneer*. His wife, Halima, was cook. Mabruki and Gardner, engaged in 1866, were from a home at Nasik in Western India where African boys rescued from slave-traders were received and trained. They were known as " Nasik boys." The loyalty and devoted service of these attendants made a deep impression on the young American. When Stanley left Livingstone and went to the coast he sent up a party of well-chosen men to accompany Livingstone on the final stage of his journey. One of these was Jacob Wainwright, a Nasik boy, of whom we shall hear again.

On August 25th, 1872, began the last lap of the great explorer's journeys. He went from Unyanyembe, where Stanley left him, southward by the borders of Lake Tanganyika to the streams and spongy swamps round Lake Bangweolo. With unflagging fortitude the party pressed on till Livingstone's strength finally gave way. With infinite care and tenderness the suffering man was borne by his African friends to Chitambo's village in Ilala. All the world knows how in the early morning of May 1st, 1873, Susi, Chuma, and three others were summoned in haste to their master. Majwara, the faithful Uganda lad who had been on duty through the night, had found Livingstone kneeling by his bedside, dead.

With wisdom and quiet courage the men took their resolve. Cost what it might, the body of their great leader should not rest in an unknown grave. It was right, though indeed it was well-nigh impossible, that they should bear it to the coast. The chief Chitambo quickly divined what had happened. He stood their friend. All honour was shown in African fashion to the dead. A little group of huts was built in a stockade outside the village. There the worn body was with reverence prepared for its long journey. Close watch was kept by day and by night. The heart was buried beneath a large mvula tree on which Jacob Wainwright carved the name and date. In the presence of all part of the Burial Service was read. Bark stripped from a myonga tree formed a cylinder in which the body was placed.

Within three weeks the little retinue set out, Majwara bearing in front the flag of England, the Union Jack. The flag of Zanzibar was also flown. They marched eastward and northward round Bangweolo towards the Luapula. Serious illness detained them for a month on the way. When they reached the broad dark river a friendly chief offered canoes to ferry them across. With all the varying fortunes of African travel they passed from place to place, camping outside an unfriendly village, camping inside one when they could, always guarding the sacred burden which they bore. Once, through an unwitting act of Amoda's, they were involved in actual fighting. Once they had to cross a mountain range. Most of the way was unknown to them all.

Nearing Unyanyembe they heard that Livingstone's son, Oswell, was there, coming to seek his father. Chuma was sent on with a full account of his illness and death, which Jacob Wainwright wrote. But Stanley had previously met the party. Hearing of his father's safety and of his determination to stay another year in Africa, Oswell Livingstone had gone home. Moving towards the coast a new peril beset the faithful group. News of the passing of Livingstone's body spread along the main road swiftly. It was unwelcome to some of the tribes. The whole plan was in jeopardy. Must the great explorer be buried in Africa after all?

The resources of the African bearers did not fail. Carefully and reverently a new arrangement was made by which the body was packed in what looked like an ordinary travelling bale. Then a faggot of mapira stalks was swathed to look like a long body ready for burial. At sundown carriers started back with the supposed body on the road towards Unyanyembe, as if the burial were to be there. When far enough from the village they dismantled the burden and scattered its parts. Then leaping into the long grass to conceal the marks of their footsteps they made their way back to the village after dark. No one discovered what they had done.

At last—how long the way must have seemed to the faithful guardians with their cherished burden!—the coast town of Bagamoyo was reached. The body of the great explorer passed from African hands and was swiftly borne to England. The whole world listened to the story of that long last march. The journey from Chitambo's village to Bagamoyo had taken from May, 1873, to February, 1874.

SCENES IN ENGLAND

The one who here tells this story stood recently in the nave of Westminster Abbey, where Livingstone's body rests among the great men of his race. The afternoon sun caught the letters on the marble slab in the pavement until they burned like gold. " It is the greatest grave in the Abbey," said a stranger who stood by. The inscription, matchless in its simplicity, sums up the man and his African friends—his devotion to work, his passionate horror of the slave-trade, his link with a chief who was kind to him and with the faithful ones who bore him to the coast.

BROUGHT BY FAITHFUL HANDS
OVER LAND AND SEA
HERE RESTS
DAVID LIVINGSTONE
MISSIONARY
TRAVELLER
PHILANTHROPIST
BORN MARCH 19, 1813
AT BLANTYRE, LANARKSHIRE
DIED MAY 1, 1873
AT CHITAMBO'S VILLAGE, ULALA.

FOR THIRTY YEARS HIS LIFE WAS SPENT
IN AN UNMEASURED EFFORT
TO EVANGELIZE THE NATIVE RACES
TO EXPLORE THE UNDISCOVERED SECRETS
TO ABOLISH THE DEVASTATING SLAVE TRADE
OF CENTRAL AFRICA
WHERE WITH HIS LATEST BREATH HE WROTE

" ALL I CAN ADD IN MY SOLITUDE IS
MAY HEAVEN'S RICH BLESSING COME DOWN
ON EVERY ONE, AMERICAN, ENGLISH OR TURK
WHO WILL HELP TO HEAL
THIS OPEN SORE OF THE WORLD."

When thousands thronged the Abbey to do honour to Livingstone on his funeral day, the pall bearers were all friends of his African journeys, men who had shared in his love for the land. Among them was the dark face of Jacob Wainwright, who had been among the explorer's servants for the closing months of his life.[1]

*　　　*　　　*　　　*　　　*　　　*

One last glimpse of two of Livingstone's African friends. It is June in England. In a lovely country house near

[1] Some people who knew of Jacob Wainwright, because he was a Nasik boy, telegraphed to invite him to come to England with the body. Susi and Chuma, who were much longer in Livingstone's service, were not known to them. They came a little later.

Nottingham, called Newstead Abbey, a group of persons waits in the beautiful flower-scented drawing-room for expected guests. There is Mrs. Webb, the gracious mistress and hostess, and her husband, long a friend of David Livingstone and an African hunter of note. There is a clergyman named Waller, about to prepare Livingstone's last journal for publication, and also Agnes, Livingstone's much-loved daughter, and Thomas his son. Newstead Abbey had been like Livingstone's English home.

The door opens. In come two pleasant-faced Africans, in thick dark-blue jackets, for to them the English summer day is cold. Introductions are quickly made. Both men have known the clergyman when he was a missionary on the Shire and Zambezi. They look with reverence at the children of their great leader and friend. In a few minutes they pass on to be cared for by the kind-hearted old housekeeper, the good butler, the family nurse, and the household staff of Newstead Abbey. Those who ministered to Livingstone in Africa and in England were quickly friends. Susi and Chuma—for it was they who had arrived—spoke English fairly and soon fell in with English ways.

One of the Newstead daughters, then only a child, has given a charming picture of the visit of the two Africans to her home. Susi, she tells us, was older and taller than Chuma, he had rather a lined and careworn face slightly marked by small-pox. Chuma was smooth-skinned, rather lighter in colour, and more vivacious with bright, dancing eyes. The two men were evidently great friends. Chuma, though much quicker in perception, made it clear that he looked up to Susi as the responsible leader. Both men were sincere Christians in all their words and ways. They looked for no praise and sought for no money beyond their wages. They won golden opinions everywhere.

They were shown the large sunny room, with its huge four-poster bed with vivid red hangings, in which Livingstone had slept, and the large black carved table at which he wrote the book about his first journey. The weather was glorious and the garden was a blaze of flowers. In the afternoons they went for walks with Tom Livingstone, discussing with him the strangeness of English ways. In the mornings they worked with Mr. Waller, often out on the grass near the lake, or under the trees. They helped to explain things that were not clear in the journal, and especially went over the details of the last days. People were impressed with the simplicity and clearness of their answers. Susi, in particular, was a geographer of no mean order. Once when there was doubt about a watershed he drew an excellent plan of the whole system of rivers. Later on, in another friend's house, when questions were asked about the hut in which Livingstone died, Susi and Chuma went out and built one just like it in an English hayfield.

Shortly after both men returned to Zanzibar.

Sekhome was very angry and he made his anger felt. He won two of his younger sons to his side and announced that he would leave all his property to them. He turned against the missionaries and the Christians. He also tried to force Khama to take a second wife. Years before Sekhome had arranged a marriage for Khama with the daughter of a great sorcerer. The cattle had been paid. Khama had never consented to the arrangement, and now Ma-Bessie was his loyal and loving wife. Yet Sekhome decreed that she must be turned into the second, inferior wife. Khama stood firm and spoke out.

I refuse on account of the word of God to take a second wife. You know I was always averse to this woman, having refused to receive her from you before I became a Christian. I thought you had given up the match. I understood you to say, before your mind was poisoned against me, that you were satisfied with my present wife. Lay the hardest task upon me with reference to hunting elephants for ivory, or any service you can think of as a token of my obedience. But I cannot take the daughter of Pelutona to wife.

Sekhome and some of his headmen were determined to end such resistance to the ways of the tribe. Khama and Khamane and all who followed them must be killed, or banished at the least. The night set for the deed came. Sekhome gathered his men round the young chiefs' huts. The order was given to fire. " Upon whom ? " asked the soldiers. " Upon those huts," cried the chief. But not a man obeyed. Sekhome raised his own double-barrelled rifle to fire, but a headman laid forcible hold of it. Then Sekhome saw that the hearts of the Bamangwato were not with him. By the custom of the tribe his life was forfeit to his sons. He fled in terror and hid in an outhouse. But his sons sent courteous messages of forgiveness to him ; he on his side promised that Khama should not be forced to take another wife.

A short time after Sekhome began to plot again. He had failed to conquer Khama ; perhaps Macheng, who was still living in banishment, would have better success. So

KHAMA

WHY are some men good and others bad ? Why are some men weak and helpless while others are strong and do useful work ? It is important to find a right answer to this question. No one wishes to be wicked or weak.

One answer often given to-day is dangerous and misleading. It kills hope and effort and leaves men to despair. There are people who state loudly that goodness and badness depend entirely on a man's surroundings, and on the sort of forefathers he has had. They say, " A man cannot help himself. His start in life fixes what he is and does. His own choice and will do not affect his future." If you speak to them of God, they say He does not interfere in human history. They do not believe that the life of an individual or of a nation is ever shaped by Him. To prove that such people are wrong in their opinions, turn to the story of Khama, Chief of the Bamangwato tribe. He began with all the odds against him, yet he grew to be good and great.

KHAMA'S START IN LIFE

For generations before his birth, Khama's ancestors dwelt in the midst of division and strife. The Bechuana tribe was part of the great wave of Bantu people who poured into South Africa, flooding the plains south of the Zambezi. Ere long the Bechuana divided into four tribes, of whom the Bakwena—the sons of the crocodile—were one.[1] These

[1] Sechele, Livingstone's friend, was the first Christian chief of the Bakwena.

Bakwena settled near the source of the Limpopo river, and soon began to break into parts again. According to their traditions one of the early chiefs, Masilo, had a quarrel with his son Malope ; Malope, in consequence, went off with part of the tribe. Malope in turn had three sons, and on his death they quarrelled and divided his portion of the tribe into three. Thus the Bakwena had become four tribes. One of these was the Bamangwato, of which Khama later on became chief. This tribe chose as their totem animal the duiker or *phuti*—a species of gazelle. They were sometimes known as the Baphuti.

The written records of the Bamangwato tribe began with Khari, the grandfather of Khama the Great. He was a vigorous and able chief who built up the fortunes of his tribe. But his three sons plunged into quarrels on his death. Sekhome, Khama's father, was determined to be chief. So he secured the murder of one brother who stood in his way. He was preparing to murder the other, Macheng, who had a prior right to the chieftainship, but Macheng fled for his life. He came back afterwards and took a large place in Khama's story, as we shall see.

Khama was born in 1827 or the following year. In his early years he suffered for the misdeeds of his ancestors. There is no record of happy boyhood for him. Family and tribal dissension beset his path. His father, Sekhome, was not respected, either as a man or as a chief. He was a great rain-maker and was feared because of his sorceries. The diviners were his allies. He invited missionaries to live in Shoshong, his capital ; he knew Livingstone and other great and good white men. He let his sons go to the mission school. But he himself clung to the old ways, keeping his mind and heart closed against good influences. Sometimes he set himself bitterly against young Khama ; at other times he was proud of his knowledge and character. " Khama has a white heart," he said to the missionary one day.

So the boy grew up. At twenty years of age he was a splendid man, over six feet in height, strong, lithe, and athletic. He was the swiftest runner, the most daring and skilful hunter, the wisest and bravest of the young warriors

of the tribe. He was a passionate lover of horses and well. His activity lasted to the end of his days.

FATHER AGAINST SON

In 1862 Khama was baptised as a member of the Chris Church. A few weeks later he married a Christian daughter of a leading man in the tribe. He and Moga mocwasele—or Ma-Bessie as she was generally call had several children and lived in happy fellowship for twe seven years. Khama needed comfort and peace in home, for he had little outside it.

He was not a man of bloodshed or war. He fought o and harder battles. But when need arose Khama was a soldier. A year after his marriage the fierce Matabele, u Lobengula, attacked the Bamangwato. Sekhome, sorc as well as commander-in-chief, went about working s[Khama suggested that it was no time for worthless m It was the time to fight. So Sekhome bade the young go forward with his regiment of some two hundred men a his own age. Only eight of them had horses. Of course little force was outnumbered and defeated. But so was Khama's resistance that the Matabele withdrew never returned. " The Bamangwato are dogs," they " but Khama is a man."

The town of Shoshong was divided. Sekhome, with twelve wives and all their relations, held fast to the old and practised the old incantations. Khama and his bro Khamane, with their young Christian wives, had m followers who looked towards the new day. In the sp of 1865 the time came round for the great *boguera* (in tion) ceremony in Shoshong. It was the custom for headmen to march to it accompanied by their sons. Kh knew from his own experience what these ceremonies like. Ma-Bessie had been through the ceremony for g Khama and Khamane had resolved to take no part in t again. So Sekhome had to march alone. His elder would not join him ; his younger sons were in school. meant open disgrace for the Chief.

Sekhome in his rage sent to invite Macheng to return to be chief in Shoshong, on condition that he put Khama and Khamane to death. While Macheng was considering this invitation, and hesitating because he did not trust Sekhome's good faith, further plots against Khama and his brother were laid.

One night a great blaze of light startled Khama from slumber. Was his home on fire? He hastened to the door, and there, just outside the hedge with which his courtyard was surrounded, he saw a group of *baloi* or wizards, working their enchantments, casting charm after charm, plant after plant, into the blazing fire, muttering dark prayers and curses against him. He stooped and crept across the court-yard till he was quite close. Then he suddenly rose to his full height inside the hedge. The wizards fled panic-stricken, leaving their spells and charms hissing in the flames. Khama put out the fire and went back to sleep.

Three months later Sekhome went to work again. By the force of his necromancy he had now bound many Bamangwato to him and he was furious with his son. Khama was warned secretly that plans against his life were ripe. That night when he was returning to his house he found armed men gathering round it. He slipped away and crossed the river; his brother Khamane joined him. They, their friends, and their cattle moved to a secure place on the mountain east of Shoshong. Sekhome's cattle were driven westward for safety. The missionary remained in the town mid-way between the combatants. For six weeks intermittent warfare went on. The Christians were nearly all on the mountain with Khama. The missionary boldly confronted Sekhome and won permission to visit his flock every day.

Khama and his party did not provoke attack. The fury of Sekhome and his party gradually cooled. At last an agreement was arrived at, and Khama returned as the recognised heir. But the healing of the breach was only on the surface. Sekhome's anger was hidden, but it was not dead. Through all these feuds Khama was wonderfully patient and forgiving. A British general who watched him at this time wrote afterwards : " He showed a Christian strength of character, humbleness of mind, patience, and generosity that clearly signalled him as a leader of men. He reminded us of the conduct of David when pursued by King Saul."

UNCLE AGAINST NEPHEW

Khama was scarcely settled back in Shoshong when his uncle Macheng appeared on the scene, to Sekhome's dismay. The old Chief no longer wanted him, but Macheng declined to be put off. He accepted the legal chieftainship which had been offered him. He would not even share it with Sekhome. Khama told his uncle in open council that the new plan could not work. He refused to be a party to it. He would simply step aside. " My kingdom," he said, " consists in my guns, my horses, and my wagon. If you will give me leave to possess these as a private person, I renounce all share in the politics of the town. I am sorry, Macheng, that I cannot give you a better welcome to the Bamangwato." Macheng told Sekhome plainly that he would not murder his nephews. He spoke in the *kotla* one day—" You called me from the Bakwena to kill your rebellious sons. My heart refuses to do this. They are your sons, not mine ; if you wish them to be killed, kill them yourself."

No one expected Sekhome to live quietly under the rule of Macheng. He called secret councils ; he worked charms and incantations ; he began to lay plots again. Some of the old men favoured his cause. He made a plan to massacre Macheng and all his supporters at a great tribal assembly. But Khama heard of his purpose and warned Macheng. Sekhome gave the signal for the attack, but there was no response. His friends warned him to flee as his life was forfeit, this time not to generous Khama but to Macheng. That evening a solitary fugitive crept down the mountain into the house of John Mackenzie, the missionary. Often as he had threatened and misjudged the white teacher, Sekhome knew that he would find shelter and food. A few hours later, with three or four attendants, he fled in the darkness to take refuge in another tribe.

Even yet, peace had not come to find a home in Shoshong. Macheng dealt fairly by his nephews at first. Then he grew jealous of them. Sekhome had been right after all; they must be put to death. Charms and incantations he tried in vain. Poison might do the work. He offered ivory to a worthless white trader in exchange for strychnine, which was used to poison wolves. The trader took the ivory, but suspecting some evil intention sent some marking ink to the Chief. Macheng bid his wife invite his nephews to drink coffee with him. They prudently declined to come. So the efficacy of marking ink as a poison was not tried. At any rate, in a coffee supper it would certainly not have been wholesome fare.

Things went from bad to worse in the tribe. Macheng was unable to rule. At last Khama appealed on behalf of the Bamangwato to Sechele, Chief of the Bakwena, who was his friend. He sent soldiers with orders to remove Macheng from the chieftainship and have him shot. To the shooting of his uncle, Khama would not consent. But Macheng, helpless from fright, was driven from the town and clambered up the mountain. No one followed him; he lived among strangers till he drank himself to death.

Thus Khama became Chief of the Bamangwato, being elected by the headmen of the tribe in September, 1872.

KHAMA'S REFORMS

A further spell of family trouble lay before Khama. His brother Khamane grew jealous of him and relations between them became strained. Then, for some reason no one has discovered, Khama invited Sekhome back to Shoshong. Did he think that the old man had learned his lesson? Did he feel that a Christian son should not leave his father in banishment? Who can say? Sechele thought the invitation an unwise one, but Sekhome accepted it at once. The old miserable plotting began again in Shoshong. At last, when one insult after another had been heaped upon him,

Khama's anger rose. He quietly withdrew from the place.

Khama marched to Serowe, some seventy miles to the north-east. Those who wished for his chieftainship could follow him, he said. There was a breathless pause in Shoshong. Then began a trek of men, women, and children after Khama, until there were five thousand empty huts in the city and all the best of the tribe were hastening to their chosen chief. Shoshong was not a pleasant place during the ensuing months, when Sekhome and Khamane ruled. Things went from bad to worse. Then Khama and all his people suddenly returned. There was short, sharp fighting. Sekhome and Khamane fled. Khama's struggle was over for the present ; he was Paramount Chief.

The time for reforms had come. Khama loved the customs of his forefathers. He was a Bamangwato through and through. Yet there were things in his tribal life which belonged to a past which were better forgotten. His totem animal were the duiker, but why should it be treated with superstitious awe ? Sekhome would not set foot on a mat of duiker skin. That was a bondage which offended Khama's manhood ; he ate duiker steak. Individual members of the tribe might continue circumcision if they wished it, but Khama withdrew the sanction of the chief. He abolished the official schools with initiation rites for boys and girls. Rain-makers he would not punish ; rain-making he did not attempt to forbid. But he let it be known that he had no faith in this or any other kind of magic, and refused to give it countenance in any way.

In ceremonies where Khama took part no heathen practices were permitted. The *kotla* saw nothing but Christian services from the day he became Chief. At seed-time and harvest there were tribal ceremonies without which it was said that rain would not fall nor seed bear fruit. At these magic was freely used. Khama had new and beautiful services arranged for the people, in which they gave thanks to God as the Father of themselves and of their race.

Khama himself had one wife. He believed in the Christian ideal of marriage and home for Africa. He could not force this on the Bamangwato, but he lived it and taught it. He strove to raise the place of women in the tribe. He had to face the opposition of some who liked the old way of life. But Khama did not mind what others thought when he saw his duty. He could stand alone against a crowd. After a few years of this enlightened rule, a white resident in Shoshong wrote :

Out of the ruins of anarchy, lawlessness, and disorder, Khama has been building up law, order, and stability. His people are living in peace. His fields are laden with corn. The white man's home is as sacred as in his own country. A purer morality is growing up from day to day. Contrasted with the past history of life at Shoshong there is a light of glory lying along the hills.

Above all things Khama feared the curse of drink for his people. " I dread it more than the assegais of the Matabele," he said. He fought against drink from the day he became Chief to the end of his life. First he stood against imported spirits. Then he prohibited the brewing of any kind of Kaffir beer.

One famous story shows the determination of the Chief. There were certain white traders in Shoshong who were quite at home under the rule of Sekhome, but they did not fit in with Khama's way at all. In later days Khama's own traders were honoured and trusted friends, to whom he did many generous kindnesses. But Sekhome's traders were as a thorn in his side. Khama had made known to all men his law against the importation of spirits. Some of the white traders, who drank freely themselves and sold liquor to the people, protested. Khama refused to yield. They tried to get supplies secretly ; Khama found them out. He told them plainly that he would make no relaxation in his law.

In defiance of Khama's orders, and hoping to get the law annulled, a party of the white traders met together one Saturday night to carouse. When they were roaring drunk they fought. Khama heard of what was happening. He went down himself, taking his missionary with him, and saw the disgraceful scene. The men were too helpless in drunken degradation to be dealt with then.

On Monday morning he summoned them before him. He was quiet, stern, and resolved. They admitted knowledge of his law. They knew he had warned them that disobedience would lead to banishment. But they begged for pity. It would ruin their business if they were sent away. Khama spoke grave, just words. He could not afford to pity them because the people God had given him needed his pity more. The traders were welcome to remove all their goods, even the corrugated iron roofing off their houses. But out of Khama's country they must go, never to return.

I am black, but I am Chief of my own country. . . . When you white men rule in the country then you can do as you like. At present I rule and shall maintain my laws. . . . You have insulted and despised me in my own town because I am a black man. . . . Take all that is yours and go. . . . I want no one but friends in my town. . . . You ought to be ashamed of yourselves. . . . I make an end of it to-day. Take your cattle ; leave my town ; never come back again.

Fifty Years of Rule

To a man like Khama it was no light thing to be chief. He had a finely tempered sense of justice which made him generous to the views of other people. But his conscience was enlightened. It compelled him to do what he felt to be right. There was bound to be active rule wherever Khama was chief. For years he had studied his people, that he might know how to govern well. Even the despised Bushmen and the dwellers in the Kalahari Desert had a place in his care. He called them " my people." Others often spoke of them as " dogs." He stopped all raiding and even theft within his territory. Traders and travellers ceased to set a watch round their waggons at night when they reached Khama's ground.

Khama, like Moshoeshoe, desired the protection of the British Government for his people. He obtained it in 1885. He was able to keep certain rights of self-government ; he also secured the maintenance of tribal laws. But the

KHAMA

WHY are some men good and others bad? Why are some men weak and helpless while others are strong and do useful work? It is important to find a right answer to this question. No one wishes to be wicked or weak.

One answer often given to-day is dangerous and misleading. It kills hope and effort and leaves men to despair. There are people who state loudly that goodness and badness depend entirely on a man's surroundings, and on the sort of forefathers he has had. They say, " A man cannot help himself. His start in life fixes what he is and does. His own choice and will do not affect his future." If you speak to them of God, they say He does not interfere in human history. They do not believe that the life of an individual or of a nation is ever shaped by Him. To prove that such people are wrong in their opinions, turn to the story of Khama, Chief of the Bamangwato tribe. He began with all the odds against him, yet he grew to be good and great.

KHAMA'S START IN LIFE

For generations before his birth, Khama's ancestors dwelt in the midst of division and strife. The Bechuana tribe was part of the great wave of Bantu people who poured into South Africa, flooding the plains south of the Zambezi. Ere long the Bechuana divided into four tribes, of whom the Bakwena—the sons of the crocodile—were one.[1] These

[1] Sechele, Livingstone's friend, was the first Christian chief of the Bakwena.

Bakwena settled near the source of the Limpopo river, and soon began to break into parts again. According to their traditions one of the early chiefs, Masilo, had a quarrel with his son Malope ; Malope, in consequence, went off with part of the tribe. Malope in turn had three sons, and on his death they quarrelled and divided his portion of the tribe into three. Thus the Bakwena had become four tribes. One of these was the Bamangwato, of which Khama later on became chief. This tribe chose as their totem animal the duiker or *phuti*—a species of gazelle. They were sometimes known as the Baphuti.

The written records of the Bamangwato tribe began with Khari, the grandfather of Khama the Great. He was a vigorous and able chief who built up the fortunes of his tribe. But his three sons plunged into quarrels on his death. Sekhome, Khama's father, was determined to be chief. So he secured the murder of one brother who stood in his way. He was preparing to murder the other, Macheng, who had a prior right to the chieftainship, but Macheng fled for his life. He came back afterwards and took a large place in Khama's story, as we shall see.

Khama was born in 1827 or the following year. In his early years he suffered for the misdeeds of his ancestors. There is no record of happy boyhood for him. Family and tribal dissension beset his path. His father, Sekhome, was not respected, either as a man or as a chief. He was a great rain-maker and was feared because of his sorceries. The diviners were his allies. He invited missionaries to live in Shoshong, his capital ; he knew Livingstone and other great and good white men. He let his sons go to the mission school. But he himself clung to the old ways, keeping his mind and heart closed against good influences. Sometimes he set himself bitterly against young Khama ; at other times he was proud of his knowledge and character. " Khama has a white heart," he said to the missionary one day.

So the boy grew up. At twenty years of age he was a splendid man, over six feet in height, strong, lithe, and athletic. He was the swiftest runner, the most daring and skilful hunter, the wisest and bravest of the young warriors of the tribe. He was a passionate lover of horses and rode well. His activity lasted to the end of his days.

FATHER AGAINST SON

In 1862 Khama was baptised as a member of the Christian Church. A few weeks later he married a Christian girl, daughter of a leading man in the tribe. He and Mogatsu-mocwasele—or Ma-Bessie as she was generally called—had several children and lived in happy fellowship for twenty-seven years. Khama needed comfort and peace in his home, for he had little outside it.

He was not a man of bloodshed or war. He fought other and harder battles. But when need arose Khama was a good soldier. A year after his marriage the fierce Matabele, under Lobengula, attacked the Bamangwato. Sekhome, sorcerer as well as commander-in-chief, went about working spells. Khama suggested that it was no time for worthless magic. It was the time to fight. So Sekhome bade the young chief go forward with his regiment of some two hundred men about his own age. Only eight of them had horses. Of course, the little force was outnumbered and defeated. But so stout was Khama's resistance that the Matabele withdrew and never returned. "The Bamangwato are dogs," they said, "but Khama is a man."

The town of Shoshong was divided. Sekhome, with his twelve wives and all their relations, held fast to the old ways and practised the old incantations. Khama and his brother Khamane, with their young Christian wives, had many followers who looked towards the new day. In the spring of 1865 the time came round for the great *boguera* (initiation) ceremony in Shoshong. It was the custom for the headmen to march to it accompanied by their sons. Khama knew from his own experience what these ceremonies were like. Ma-Bessie had been through the ceremony for girls. Khama and Khamane had resolved to take no part in them again. So Sekhome had to march alone. His elder sons would not join him; his younger sons were in school. It meant open disgrace for the Chief.

Sekhome was very angry and he made his anger felt. He won two of his younger sons to his side and announced that he would leave all his property to them. He turned against the missionaries and the Christians. He also tried to force Khama to take a second wife. Years before Sekhome had arranged a marriage for Khama with the daughter of a great sorcerer. The cattle had been paid. Khama had never consented to the arrangement, and now Ma-Bessie was his loyal and loving wife. Yet Sekhome decreed that she must be turned into the second, inferior wife. Khama stood firm and spoke out.

I refuse on account of the word of God to take a second wife. You know I was always averse to this woman, having refused to receive her from you before I became a Christian. I thought you had given up the match. I understood you to say, before your mind was poisoned against me, that you were satisfied with my present wife. Lay the hardest task upon me with reference to hunting elephants for ivory, or any service you can think of as a token of my obedience. But I cannot take the daughter of Pelutona to wife.

Sekhome and some of his headmen were determined to end such resistance to the ways of the tribe. Khama and Khamane and all who followed them must be killed, or banished at the least. The night set for the deed came. Sekhome gathered his men round the young chiefs' huts. The order was given to fire. " Upon whom ? " asked the soldiers. " Upon those huts," cried the chief. But not a man obeyed. Sekhome raised his own double-barrelled rifle to fire, but a headman laid forcible hold of it. Then Sekhome saw that the hearts of the Bamangwato were not with him. By the custom of the tribe his life was forfeit to his sons. He fled in terror and hid in an outhouse. But his sons sent courteous messages of forgiveness to him ; he on his side promised that Khama should not be forced to take another wife.

A short time after Sekhome began to plot again. He had failed to conquer Khama ; perhaps Macheng, who was still living in banishment, would have better success. So

Sekhome in his rage sent to invite Macheng to return to be chief in Shoshong, on condition that he put Khama and Khamane to death. While Macheng was considering this invitation, and hesitating because he did not trust Sekhome's good faith, further plots against Khama and his brother were laid.

One night a great blaze of light startled Khama from slumber. Was his home on fire? He hastened to the door, and there, just outside the hedge with which his courtyard was surrounded, he saw a group of *baloi* or wizards, working their enchantments, casting charm after charm, plant after plant, into the blazing fire, muttering dark prayers and curses against him. He stooped and crept across the courtyard till he was quite close. Then he suddenly rose to his full height inside the hedge. The wizards fled panic-stricken, leaving their spells and charms hissing in the flames. Khama put out the fire and went back to sleep.

Three months later Sekhome went to work again. By the force of his necromancy he had now bound many Bamangwato to him and he was furious with his son. Khama was warned secretly that plans against his life were ripe. That night when he was returning to his house he found armed men gathering round it. He slipped away and crossed the river; his brother Khamane joined him. They, their friends, and their cattle moved to a secure place on the mountain east of Shoshong. Sekhome's cattle were driven westward for safety. The missionary remained in the town mid-way between the combatants. For six weeks intermittent warfare went on. The Christians were nearly all on the mountain with Khama. The missionary boldly confronted Sekhome and won permission to visit his flock every day.

Khama and his party did not provoke attack. The fury of Sekhome and his party gradually cooled. At last an agreement was arrived at, and Khama returned as the recognised heir. But the healing of the breach was only on the surface. Sekhome's anger was hidden, but it was not dead. Through all these feuds Khama was wonderfully patient and forgiving. A British general who watched him

at this time wrote afterwards : "He showed a Christian
strength of character, humbleness of mind, patience, and
generosity that clearly signalled him as a leader of men.
He reminded us of the conduct of David when pursued by
King Saul."

Uncle against Nephew

Khama was scarcely settled back in Shoshong when his
uncle Macheng appeared on the scene, to Sekhome's dismay.
The old Chief no longer wanted him, but Macheng declined
to be put off. He accepted the legal chieftainship which
had been offered him. He would not even share it with
Sekhome. Khama told his uncle in open council that the
new plan could not work. He refused to be a party to it.
He would simply step aside. "My kingdom," he said,
"consists in my guns, my horses, and my wagon. If you
will give me leave to possess these as a private person, I
renounce all share in the politics of the town. I am sorry,
Macheng, that I cannot give you a better welcome to the
Bamangwato." Macheng told Sekhome plainly that he
would not murder his nephews. He spoke in the *kotla* one
day—"You called me from the Bakwena to kill your
rebellious sons. My heart refuses to do this. They are your
sons, not mine ; if you wish them to be killed, kill them
yourself."

No one expected Sekhome to live quietly under the rule
of Macheng. He called secret councils ; he worked charms
and incantations ; he began to lay plots again. Some of
the old men favoured his cause. He made a plan to
massacre Macheng and all his supporters at a great tribal
assembly. But Khama heard of his purpose and warned
Macheng. Sekhome gave the signal for the attack, but there
was no response. His friends warned him to flee as his life
was forfeit, this time not to generous Khama but to
Macheng. That evening a solitary fugitive crept down the
mountain into the house of John Mackenzie, the missionary.
Often as he had threatened and misjudged the white teacher,
Sekhome knew that he would find shelter and food. A few

hours later, with three or four attendants, he fled in the darkness to take refuge in another tribe.

Even yet, peace had not come to find a home in Shoshong. Macheng dealt fairly by his nephews at first. Then he grew jealous of them. Sekhome had been right after all; they must be put to death. Charms and incantations he tried in vain. Poison might do the work. He offered ivory to a worthless white trader in exchange for strychnine, which was used to poison wolves. The trader took the ivory, but suspecting some evil intention sent some marking ink to the Chief. Macheng bid his wife invite his nephews to drink coffee with him. They prudently declined to come. So the efficacy of marking ink as a poison was not tried. At any rate, in a coffee supper it would certainly not have been wholesome fare.

Things went from bad to worse in the tribe. Macheng was unable to rule. At last Khama appealed on behalf of the Bamangwato to Sechele, Chief of the Bakwena, who was his friend. He sent soldiers with orders to remove Macheng from the chieftainship and have him shot. To the shooting of his uncle, Khama would not consent. But Macheng, helpless from fright, was driven from the town and clambered up the mountain. No one followed him; he lived among strangers till he drank himself to death.

Thus Khama became Chief of the Bamangwato, being elected by the headmen of the tribe in September, 1872.

KHAMA'S REFORMS

A further spell of family trouble lay before Khama. His brother Khamane grew jealous of him and relations between them became strained. Then, for some reason no one has discovered, Khama invited Sekhome back to Shoshong. Did he think that the old man had learned his lesson? Did he feel that a Christian son should not leave his father in banishment? Who can say? Sechele thought the invitation an unwise one, but Sekhome accepted it at once. The old miserable plotting began again in Shoshong. At last, when one insult after another had been heaped upon him,

Khama's anger rose. He quietly withdrew from the place.

Khama marched to Serowe, some seventy miles to the north-east. Those who wished for his chieftainship could follow him, he said. There was a breathless pause in Shoshong. Then began a trek of men, women, and children after Khama, until there were five thousand empty huts in the city and all the best of the tribe were hastening to their chosen chief. Shoshong was not a pleasant place during the ensuing months, when Sekhome and Khamane ruled. Things went from bad to worse. Then Khama and all his people suddenly returned. There was short, sharp fighting. Sekhome and Khamane fled. Khama's struggle was over for the present ; he was Paramount Chief.

The time for reforms had come. Khama loved the customs of his forefathers. He was a Bamangwato through and through. Yet there were things in his tribal life which belonged to a past which were better forgotten. His totem animal were the duiker, but why should it be treated with superstitious awe ? Sekhome would not set foot on a mat of duiker skin. That was a bondage which offended Khama's manhood ; he ate duiker steak. Individual members of the tribe might continue circumcision if they wished it, but Khama withdrew the sanction of the chief. He abolished the official schools with initiation rites for boys and girls. Rain-makers he would not punish ; rain-making he did not attempt to forbid. But he let it be known that he had no faith in this or any other kind of magic, and refused to give it countenance in any way.

In ceremonies where Khama took part no heathen practices were permitted. The *kotla* saw nothing but Christian services from the day he became Chief. At seed-time and harvest there were tribal ceremonies without which it was said that rain would not fall nor seed bear fruit. At these magic was freely used. Khama had new and beautiful services arranged for the people, in which they gave thanks to God as the Father of themselves and of their race.

Khama himself had one wife. He believed in the Christian ideal of marriage and home for Africa. He could

not force this on the Bamangwato, but he lived it and taught
it. He strove to raise the place of women in the tribe.
He had to face the opposition of some who liked the old
way of life. But Khama did not mind what others thought
when he saw his duty. He could stand alone against a
crowd. After a few years of this enlightened rule, a white
resident in Shoshong wrote :

Out of the ruins of anarchy, lawlessness, and disorder, Khama
has been building up law, order, and stability. His people are
living in peace. His fields are laden with corn. The white man's
home is as sacred as in his own country. A purer morality is
growing up from day to day. Contrasted with the past history
of life at Shoshong there is a light of glory lying along the hills.

Above all things Khama feared the curse of drink for
his people. " I dread it more than the assegais of the
Matabele," he said. He fought against drink from the day
he became Chief to the end of his life. First he stood against
imported spirits. Then he prohibited the brewing of any
kind of Kaffir beer.

One famous story shows the determination of the Chief.
There were certain white traders in Shoshong who were
quite at home under the rule of Sekhome, but they did not
fit in with Khama's way at all. In later days Khama's own
traders were honoured and trusted friends, to whom he did
many generous kindnesses. But Sekhome's traders were as
a thorn in his side. Khama had made known to all men his
law against the importation of spirits. Some of the white
traders, who drank freely themselves and sold liquor to the
people, protested. Khama refused to yield. They tried to
get supplies secretly ; Khama found them out. He told
them plainly that he would make no relaxation in his law.

In defiance of Khama's orders, and hoping to get the law
annulled, a party of the white traders met together one
Saturday night to carouse. When they were roaring drunk
they fought. Khama heard of what was happening. He
went down himself, taking his missionary with him, and saw
the disgraceful scene. The men were too helpless in drunken
degradation to be dealt with then.

On Monday morning he summoned them before him. He was quiet, stern, and resolved. They admitted knowledge of his law. They knew he had warned them that disobedience would lead to banishment. But they begged for pity. It would ruin their business if they were sent away. Khama spoke grave, just words. He could not afford to pity them because the people God had given him needed his pity more. The traders were welcome to remove all their goods, even the corrugated iron roofing off their houses. But out of Khama's country they must go, never to return.

I am black, but I am Chief of my own country. . . . When you white men rule in the country then you can do as you like. At present I rule and shall maintain my laws. . . . You have insulted and despised me in my own town because I am a black man. . . . Take all that is yours and go. . . . I want no one but friends in my town. . . . You ought to be ashamed of yourselves. . . . I make an end of it to-day. Take your cattle ; leave my town ; never come back again.

Fifty Years of Rule

To a man like Khama it was no light thing to be chief. He had a finely tempered sense of justice which made him generous to the views of other people. But his conscience was enlightened. It compelled him to do what he felt to be right. There was bound to be active rule wherever Khama was chief. For years he had studied his people, that he might know how to govern well. Even the despised Bushmen and the dwellers in the Kalahari Desert had a place in his care. He called them " my people." Others often spoke of them as " dogs." He stopped all raiding and even theft within his territory. Traders and travellers ceased to set a watch round their waggons at night when they reached Khama's ground.

Khama, like Moshoeshoe, desired the protection of the British Government for his people. He obtained it in 1885. He was able to keep certain rights of self-government ; he also secured the maintenance of tribal laws. But the country of the Bamangwato lay in the direct line of trade towards the north, and efforts were made to get hold of Khama's land. This the Chief strenuously withstood. In 1895 Khama, and two other chiefs, under the escort of two

KHAMA THE GOOD.
Photo by Neville Jones.

missionaries, came to England to place their case before the British Government. They won their cause. Khama made many friends in England by his charm and gentleness and the strength of his Christian manhood. Much hospitality was shown to him. He was famous for his short speeches.

His longest took about seven minutes ; his shortest, and one of his best, contained forty words.

Khama went home to find trouble awaiting him in Shoshong. His son was following in the footsteps of the grandfather whose name he bore. In 1889 the capital of the Bamangwato was moved from Shoshong to Palapye ; later still the tribe found in Serowe, where Khama had gone in his father's days, the capital which met their needs. At Palapye, Ma-Bessie died, loved and honoured by all. Khama afterwards married a fine woman named Semane, who survived him. Her son Tsekedi, in manner and presence like his father, is now regent for the boy chief of the Bamangwato, Sekhome's little son.

Who can find words to tell the story of all that happened in fifty years of rule ? Khama steadily gained confidence and honour as time rolled on. He was not faultless, of course. He could be harsh, even unjust, in his judgments. He turned away men—both black and white—who had loved and served him well. There was some ground at times for calling him obstinate and self-willed. Yet what a man he was, from first to last ! His life was crowded with incident and he never slackened pace. He was still a daring rider at ninety years of age.

After Khama's death, Lord Buxton, the second Governor-General of South Africa, published a story about Khama in the *Times* newspaper, which gives a charming picture of the Chief in his old age.

The last time I saw Khama was in August, 1920, a very few days before I left South Africa. He was a great age, and I was much touched by his insisting on making the three days' journey from Serowe to Cape Town to say good-bye. . . . He and I had an affectionate interview. . . . Towards the close my wife came into the room with our grandson in her arms—a baby of fourteen months. . . . The old man rose up, took the child in his arms, and growled and grunted his appreciation. It was rather an anxious moment ; but the little boy looked at him fearlessly, said, " Man, Man," and stroked his face. . . . That is my last impression of Khama ; the very tall, very dark South African chief, holding in his arms the very small, very fair English child.

Three Scenes in Serowe

Three great scenes at Serowe bring us to the close of the story of Khama's life.

Khama's Jubilee.—The old man, with his noble presence and unsullied character, has been Chief of the Bamangwato for fifty years. It is summer time in the year 1922 and great celebrations are being held in Serowe. The big church is too small for the company. At least five thousand tribesmen assemble in the *kotla*. More than one hundred white people —government officials, missionaries, and traders—are seated round the old Chief's chair. One official after another pays honour to the hero of the day. The missionaries greet him with love. The regiments in bright-coloured costumes come forward in old-time barbaric splendour to acclaim him. The leader of the Yellow Regiment speaks for the tribe. He lauds the greatness of Khama's reign. And there, in the *kotla* where so many plots against Khama's religion have been made, the spokesman of the tribe acknowledges publicly that prosperity has sprung from the teaching the missionaries brought.

Then Khama, hale for all his weight of years, rises to speak. Never before has he said so many words in the *kotla*. He sends a message of loyalty and his blessing to King George V. He gives thanks for the congratulations of his white friends, especially the missionaries. He calls attention to those towns in his country which still refuse to receive missionary teachers. Then he closes with words which are still a heritage for the young men of all Africa to-day :

Let these words enter your hearts. . . . Depart from disputes ; think like men ; seek to know the road ; let your hearts depart from drink and from the initiation ceremonies ; get to know the true knowledge about marriage, that it is an oath before God. May God bless you, white people and my people.

Khama's Death.—It is a few months later—February, 1923. The great and good chief Khama, watched over by loving wife and devoted household, draws to the close of his many days. It is but a week since he filled his wonted place in the *kotla* and went for his daily ride. He was drenched in a rainstorm when on horseback and badly chilled. Now his strength fails steadily. There is no reaction towards recovery. Khama, a great peace within and around him, is quietly passing away. He knows his time has come. He has finished his course and kept the faith. There are no last messages to be given, no forgotten things to be done. Semane tells how gently the low sweet voice spoke to her. His missionary kneels beside him with all the household and prays. Ere he ceases the golden gates open—Khama the Good has died.

Khama's Great Memorial.—More than two years have passed. It is June, 1925. Sekhome, Khama's son, is nearing the end of his short, unhappy reign. But to-day men think not of him, but of the great Chief Khama, and of the Prince of Wales, son of King George V and great grandson of Queen Victoria, who has come that day to Serowe. He is there to unveil the memorial raised over Khama's rock-hewn grave on Serowe hill. A great *indaba* is being held in the *kotla*. The Prince in gracious words does fitting honour to the memory of " one of the greatest chiefs in the history of South Africa."

Then up, up the steep road lined with troops to a projecting spur of the kopje, the procession winds its way, halting in a circular space bordered by sandstone walls. There the monument stands, draped from view. Southward lie the vast plain and distant mountain ranges ; beneath the hill is Serowe, with its beehive huts and stockades. Khama's people are clustered round the place where their Chieftain's body rests. There is a brief moving service of commemoration, led by the missionaries whom Khama loved. Then the Prince releases the folds of the flag which drapes the memorial, and there stands out a beautiful white marble plinth, and on it the bronze figure of an African gazelle—the totem of Khama's tribe.

A scroll on the marble bears the inscription :

> HERE LIE THE REMAINS OF KHAMA
> " RIGHTEOUSNESS EXALTETH A NATION "

SAMUEL ADJAI CROWTHER : FROM SLAVE BOY TO BISHOP

Chicken Farmer and Boy Slave

ADJAI was born about the year 1806. He was a pure Yoruba of good family both on his father's and his mother's side. His father was a weaver—this was the family trade. He was also a farmer and a headman or councillor in Oshogun. This was a town of 12,000 inhabitants, about one hundred miles inland from Lagos. Adjai had a happy home with no time for idleness. As a little lad he kept chickens, breeding and selling them. The profit of his trade once amounted to a whole string of cowries, worth sixpence. He also grew yams on a bit of land next to his father's farm, and sold them. He was captain of a club of forty boys who all did a little farming. Adjai thought it great fun to walk seven miles to his own ground in the cool of the early morning. He turned up all the earth for his yams. Then he could sit and watch his friends hoeing while the sun was hot.

Adjai was a plucky boy. One day his father's hut took fire ; the family barely escaped. When the last child was in safety Adjai's father remembered that the household gods were on a shelf in the midst of the flames. " O my gods ! " he cried, " they will all be burned." Adjai dashed through the blazing doorway and amid the cheers of the neighbours rescued the family gods. A new home was quickly built, and Adjai settled down again to breed chickens and grow yams.

One beautiful morning early in 1821 the town lay at peace in the sunshine. In Adjai's home, as in thousands of others, breakfast was being prepared. Suddenly confusion and terror reigned. A great band of Mohammedans and Fulahs were ravaging the country to capture slaves for the Portuguese. Some of them were marching on Oshogun. Adjai's father rushed off to help in the defence of the town. There was not much hope. The fence round the town was weak in many places and there were six gates to defend. Three or four hours later Adjai's father dashed home for a moment to bid his wife and children fly for their lives. They never saw him again.

In later years Adjai wrote the story of that terrible time. Women piled their household goods into baskets, and slung their babies on their shoulders. With children clinging round them they ran out of the town to hide. But the prickly bushes tore them. They dropped their baskets and tried to save the children and themselves. It was too late. The captors put rope nooses round their necks and tied them together. A whole drove were led off by one man. The slaves were brought before the chief captor. He kept Adjai and his eldest sister for himself. Adjai's mother and baby sister went to those who had made the raid.

The lad was passed from hand to hand until, as he said, he became " a veteran in slavery." He was exchanged for a horse and bartered more than once for tobacco. He was sold in the open market and watched his price being counted out. At last the fear which had haunted him came to pass. He stood in a slave market at Lagos and was bought for tobacco once more. He was taken, stiff with terror, in a canoe across the first river he had ever seen. And white Portuguese came and examined him. " It was not without great fear and trembling," he wrote afterwards, " that I received for the first time the touch of a white hand."

The white men bought him and chained him cruelly with other slaves. They were packed like logs in an ill-ventilated room. One night one hundred and eighty-seven slaves, including Adjai, were sent in canoes to a Portuguese vessel which was waiting. Early next morning she set sail. The wretched slaves were first hungry, and then too ill to eat. They were packed down in the hold. It was the worst day

Adjai had ever known and the night which followed it was worse.

Next morning the hatches were opened. The weary, miserable slaves were summoned on deck. Oh, the fresh air and sunshine after the stifling heat down below! But what had happened in the night? There were strange white men on deck with long, alarming swords. The slave owner and the Portuguese sailors were bound. Some one was cooking breakfast: how hungry they were now! Riding on the water were two British men-of-war and several brigs. They were rescued; they were slaves no longer. But they did not understand.

Fresh terrors began. The slaves had been drawn together in their misfortune. Now they were separated into groups and sent to different ships. What were they wanted for? Adjai and five other boys stuck close together and were taken off to a man-of-war. Timidly their eyes sought for some of their companions. Not one was in sight. What was that long dead body, partly eaten, hanging from a hook? What were those round things like black heads lying on the deck of the ship? Not till the cloven hoof of the dead hog was discovered, and the black heads were found to be iron cannon balls, were the boys sure that they were not going to be eaten by the crew.

But soon all fears were passed. The captain was kind to the boys. The sailors adopted them and gave them clothes. The good ship cruised about for several weeks, picking up rescued slaves, and then set sail for Sierra Leone. Here, on June 17th, 1822, Adjai set foot again on African soil, no longer slave but free.

In Sierra Leone a special settlement called Freetown had been established for rescued slaves. There they were landed, often miserable enough, speaking many dialects, torn from home and tribe, not knowing what the future held. Some of them were broken down and feeble, almost past response to help. Others, like Adjai, only wanted a chance to step out into life. He was sent to a mission school a few miles from Freetown and fell at once upon his feet.

SCHOOL AND COLLEGE

On Adjai's first day at school another boy was set to
teach him his letters. Adjai was so fascinated that he
begged a halfpenny from a Yoruba man and bought an
alphabet card for himself. He was a quick and eager pupil.
In the evenings he did lessons at a table with one lighted
candle in the middle. At the head sat the schoolmaster's
wife. Beside Adjai sat a little Yoruba girl named Asano.
She too had been rescued from a slave ship. Years after
she became Adjai's wife.

By December, 1825, Adjai had learned to understand
and believe in the Christian message. He was baptised.
Henceforth he was known as Samuel Adjai Crowther, called
after a good old clergyman in London. The following year
two of Adjai's missionary teachers went to London. They
took the boy with them, possibly to prove that it was
worth while having schools for freed slaves in Sierra Leone.
For eight months the boy attended a parochial school in
North London, working side by side with English boys.

On returning to Sierra Leone he taught for a little in a
Government school. But his education was still slender ;
he wanted to know much more. Fourah Bay College had
just been founded by the Church Missionary Society at
Freetown to give Africans fuller training. Young Crowther
was the first student on the roll.

The lad arrived bringing a mattress for his bed. He had
been given it as a present from England. The Principal
objected ; it was a luxury unknown to the other boys. So
Crowther took it away. Presently he and four other boys
were made monitors. They were advised to wear shoes on
Sunday when they went to church. Hitherto they had gone
barefoot, but now they must live up to the dignity of their
office. Bishop Crowther's children loved to make him tell
the story of those shoes. They were rough and hard and
they hurt his feet. He could scarcely stand in them, much
less walk. And it was three miles to church on Sundays.
Finally the resolute monitors put on their shoes, clung to

the wall of the room for support, and painfully tramped round and round till their feet grew used to confinement. On Sundays they started bravely in their shoes, took them off when out of sight of the college, and put them on again when near the church.

But Adjai soon began to move towards manhood. We hear of him going to church in white stockings, shoes, a blue serge suit, a waistcoat, and a beaver hat. He was careful, he tells us, to buy boots that creaked as he walked. The Principal, who was a splendid teacher, said, " He is a lad of uncommon ability, steady conduct, a thirst for knowledge, and indefatigable industry."

Meantime some one else was growing up too. When Adjai entered Fourah Bay College he told the Principal he hoped one day to win his old school friend Asano for his wife. She too had become a Christian and been baptised, changing her pretty African name for that of Susan Thompson. By the time Adjai was assistant schoolmaster at Regent, Asano was a schoolmistress herself. They were married and had three sons and three daughters. For fifty years they lived happily together until Mrs. Crowther died at Lagos in 1881.

Adjai went back to Fourah Bay College as tutor, studying while he taught. He worked hard at Greek and Latin. He became assistant in a parish, learning to understand and meet the needs of men. He managed a large Sunday School. The time was coming when a great gateway to larger life would open before him. Adjai had honestly striven to prepare himself for this.

The Exploration of the Niger

The man who was born in the Yoruba country and educated in Sierra Leone was now to have his life linked with the mighty Niger. It was in 1841—the year in which Livingstone went to Africa—that Crowther's call to the Niger came.

Some of the secrets of the Niger were already known. Mungo Park and Clapperton had seen its majestic upper

waters before they died. In 1830 Lander had been the
first to trace its courses to the sea. No one had yet ascended
the vast waterway. It was known that slave-trading was
rife. It was believed that honest trade would check it.

A group of men in England persuaded the Government
to fit out an Expedition to the Niger. It had a threefold
aim. It was to make treaties with the tribes along the
banks. It was to induce them to promise to abandon the
slave trade. It was to help them to develop export trade.
Three iron steamers were specially built. Men of science
were engaged to go with the Expedition. Money was given
to start a model farm at some suitable site on the river.
The Church Missionary Society got leave to send two men
with the party. They chose J. F. Schön, a German
missionary at Sierra Leone who had a brilliant knowledge
of African languages. And they chose Samuel Adjai
Crowther.

In the eyes of the public, the Expedition was a disastrous
failure. The climate of the river seemed fatal to white men.
Out of one hundred and fifty Europeans, forty-two died in
two months. The three vessels got as far as the confluence
of the Niger and the Benue (or Tshadda). A site was chosen
for the model farm and men landed to begin the work. Then
one vessel had to return to the coast full of invalids. A
second had speedily to follow it. The third, with Crowther
in the party, pressed on to Egan, some three hundred and
fifty miles from the sea. But when only three white men
were left able to work the vessel, she too had to turn and
slip down on the swift current to the sea. Such men as
were still alive at the model farm were picked up as she
passed.

Among white men the Niger Expedition was called a
disaster. But Crowther saw it through African eyes. As
the ships moved up the great river and anchored, the white
men held palavers and made treaties with the chiefs.
Crowther, keen of eye and fearless in giving his message,
was off among the villages and towns. The primitive life
of the riverside villages was open to him. His African
speech stood him in good stead. He knew how to get near

the people. He made friends with kings and chiefs, with old women and children, pagan and Moslem alike. He knew he had the message which would break the bondage of the people and transform their life.

At Cape Coast Castle on the Gold Coast Crowther saw something which he never forget. He was on his way to the Niger. He found a monument to Philip Quaque, a Gold Coast Native clergyman. In that district where Europeans died off like flies this man had worked among his people for over fifty years, from 1765 to 1816. On the Niger Expedition Crowther saw one after another of his European friends sicken and die. He tended them in their suffering and stood beside their lonely graves. There grew up in his mind a great conviction that it was through Africans that the needs of West Africa could be met.

Thirteen years later the Second Niger Expedition was sent up the river, with only one ship. Crowther was on board. The expedition was a success. There was no serious illness among the members. The Benue was explored for nearly four hundred miles. Valuable links were made with the tribes. The leader of the Expedition gave Crowther credit for many of the good results. " The reception we met with all along," wrote Crowther, " from the kings and chiefs of the countries was beyond expectation. I believe the time has fully come when Christianity must be introduced on the banks of the Niger. God has provided instruments to begin the work in the liberated Africans of Sierra Leone who are Natives of the Niger territories."

The Missionary Pioneer

A new stage of Crowther's life began between the first and second expedition up the Niger.

When his *Journal* of the first expedition was published, it showed his power to do pioneer work. He was invited back to England and sent to a college for training ministers. In 1842, twenty-one years after he was rescued from slavery, he was ordained a clergyman of the Church of England. He was the first African clergyman on the lists of the Church Missionary Society. Once again Crowther proved a good student. The Bishop who ordained him said, " That man is no mean scholar. His examination papers were capital and his Latin extremely good."

Meantime interesting things had been happening in West Africa. In the Yoruba country some remnants of the Egba tribe began to gather together. They settled round a high, lonely rock with caves where they could hide. By degrees others who had escaped the slave raiders joined them. A town grew up. They called it Abeokuta or Under-stone. There were many Egba among the rescued slaves at Sierra Leone. Some of these had prospered as traders. They bought a little ship and sold English goods at ports along the coast. After a time some of these traders made their way to Abeokuta. Then large numbers of the Egba from Sierra Leone began to return and settle in their old country. In Sierra Leone the Egba had become Christians. But many of them were very ignorant still. They sent to ask for Christian teachers for themselves and for the great heathen town of Abeokuta.

Crowther, who had just been ordained, was chosen as one of the pioneers. On his way from England he stopped at Sierra Leone. What a welcome he was given ! Crowds flocked to hear " the black man who was crowned a minister " preach in English and in Yoruba. " Wherever I go the people welcome me as a messenger of Christ," he wrote. He worked at translating the Bible into the Yoruba language. He visited the Mohammedans, in whom he always took special interest. He went and sat down among the heathen worshippers, reasoning patiently with them.

The little party soon moved on to Badagry on their way to Abeokuta. But local wars had closed the road, and it was not until 1846 that the pioneers arrived at their destination. It was a pouring wet day. The travellers were soaked to the skin. But they had to go round Abeokuta to see the sights before they were taken to Sagbua the chief. A public meeting was held at which the Chief took the chair. Crowther, speaking in Yoruba, explained the purposes of the mission. A collection was taken. Sagbua gave 20,000 cowries ; everybody present gave 1,000 (2s. 6d. in English money). A piece of land was given. Women were employed to carry clay for the walls of the church. The building was soon finished and ready for work.

A wonderful thing now happened to Crowther. News came that his mother and sisters were living in a neighbouring town. He sent for them. The sisters doubted and did not come. But the old mother hastened to see if it really was her son. " When she saw me," wrote Crowther, " she trembled. She could not believe her own eyes. We grasped one another in silence and great astonishment. Big tears rolled down her emaciated cheeks. She held me by the hand and called me by the familiar names I used to be called by my grandmother. We could not say much, but sat still casting many an affectionate look at one another. I had given up all hope, and now, after a separation of twenty-five years, we were brought together again."

Crowther's heart bled as he heard the story of those years. No news of him had reached his mother. A relative redeemed her and his sisters from slavery. The sisters married, and for a time lived in peace. Then one day raiders captured his mother and her eldest daughter on the way to market. The daughter's husband ransomed her. But the poor old mother was sold in open market, sent from place to place and found herself finally in bitter bondage in Abeokuta. At last her daughter collected cowries enough to redeem her for £4 10s.

Afala—that was her name—stayed gladly with her long-lost son. She wanted to offer a special sacrifice to her gods for his restoration. But Crowther told her of the Christian's God. The English missionary who was Crowther's colleague undertook to teach her. She became a true Christian and was the first convert in the Abeokuta mission. At baptism she took the name of Hannah, because her son was called Samuel. She lived to be over one hundred years of age.

The mission work prospered in Abeokuta. In three years a strong Christian community had grown up. In

1851 a terrible danger threatened the town. Kosoko, king of Lagos, and Gezo, king of Dahomey, gathered a great army to attack Abeokuta. The Christians spent the evening praying for deliverance. Next morning they manned the mud walls and helped to defend the town. The great hosts of Dahomey were defeated and driven back. Hundreds of the famous women warriors of Dahomey were left dead upon the field.

That same year Crowther again visited England. He brought his wife with him. The importance of her work as helpmeet to her husband, and as the first Christian mother in Abeokuta, was publicly recognised. Crowther was received by the Queen and some of her ministers. At first he did not recognise the gracious lady who asked such close questions about Abeokuta and Lagos, about the slave trade and the King of Dahomey's attack. Then some one said " Your Majesty," and Crowther knew it was the Queen. During this visit to England another interesting meeting took place. Crowther sat in the Church Missionary House one day at work upon a Yoruba translation. A gentleman entered the room. Crowther looked up, threw his pen aside, and with joy embraced the surprised newcomer. It was Sir Henry Leeke, who was captain of the ship which rescued Crowther more than twenty-five years before. Crowther went to stay with his deliverer in his English country house and preached in the parish church.

Crowther and his wife returned to Africa, but a call to go on the second Expedition up the Niger (see p. 71) took him from the Abeokuta work. On his return a further call awaited him which shaped the rest of his life.

BISHOP AND SERVANT OF THE CHURCH

Henceforth it was on the Niger that Crowther found his sphere. He was commissioned to accompany the third Niger Expedition up the great river in 1857, this time as leader of the first Christian mission to the Niger. The plans were large and bold. Teachers were to be planted at centres along the river. Crowther and the leader of the expedition

hoped to travel overland from Rabbah to the great city of
Sokoto.

But just beyond Rabbah the vessel was wrecked on
hidden rocks. The travellers, short of supplies, had to wait
twelve months till another vessel came to take them down
the river. Crowther left the party at Onitsha and went up
the river again in native canoes to Rabbah. Then he
travelled on foot by an unknown way from Rabbah to Ilorin
and so to Abeokuta and Lagos.

Further journeys up and down the river followed, sometimes alone, sometimes with recruits. There were openings
everywhere for mission work. But it still seemed as if
white men could not live on the Niger. Little groups of
Christians were springing up. How were they to be supervised ? What bishop could go up and down the river to
confirm the Christians and ordain men for the ministry ?
Trained Africans were already waiting at Onitsha and
Gbebe, ready to be commissioned for fuller work. Who was
to launch them forth ?

Then Henry Venn, the statesmanlike secretary of the
Church Missionary Society, thought of a great plan. It was
a plan which crowned the long-proved Christian service of
Crowther's life. The Niger mission should be purely
African, and in Samuel Adjai Crowther its first bishop was
to be found.

To-day it seems natural to think of Africans as bishops.
Sixty years ago it was not so. No one was more surprised
than Crowther himself. In 1864, when he came to England
to report his seven years' work on the Niger, the daring
proposal was made. Humbly and repeatedly Crowther
declined it. But Henry Venn had gained the consent of
all the authorities. Every difficulty had been cleared away.
At last Crowther's consent was won. The Queen's licence
was issued, empowering the Archbishop of Canterbury to
consecrate "our trusty and well-beloved Samuel Adjai
Crowther" to be a bishop of the Church of England in West
Africa. The University of Oxford conferred the degree of
Doctor of Divinity (D.D.) upon the bishop-elect.

On St. Peter's Day, June 29th, 1864, special trains were

run from London to Canterbury. The glorious old Cathedral
was bathed in summer sunshine. The place was full of
memories. There early scenes of Christianity in England
had been enacted. Through those lofty aisles Church
leaders of all the centuries had passed. In that Cathedral
bishops had been consecrated for the Church in many lands.
But never before had a West African been sent forth from
Canterbury as a father in God to men of his own race. No
wonder that special trains were needed and that every seat
in Canterbury Cathedral was filled.

Crowther had many friends who came to be with him on
that great day. Two stand out among the rest. One was
Sir Henry Leeke, once Captain of H.M.S. *Myrmidon* which
rescued Adjai the boy slave. The other was an elderly
lady who asked for a seat where she could see and hear.
" That black minister who is to be consecrated bishop this
morning was taught the alphabet by me." When this was
known one of the best seats was gladly given. The lady
was Mrs. Weeks of Sierra Leone. The beautiful solemn
service was never more impressive than on that morning
when Samuel Adjai Crowther was consecrated for his task.

*   *   *   *   *

It is worth while to recall the events of Crowther's career.
Can a more remarkable one be found ? In 1821, a kid-
napped slave ; in 1822, a liberated African ; in 1823, a
schoolboy in Sierra Leone ; in 1825, a baptised Christian ;
in 1826, a college student ; in 1828, a teacher ; in 1841, an
explorer ; in 1843, an ordained minister ; in 1857, a pioneer
missionary to the country from which he was stolen ; in
1864, a bishop.

Crowther was consecrated in June, 1864 ; he died on the
last day of December, 1891. Over the seven and twenty
years of his episcopate many shadows passed. But gleams
of sunshine gladdened his faithful work. He went to and
fro upon the Niger, and in and out of its delta. He began
new work and strove to build up the old. The story of those
busy years is too long to tell here.

The African workers stationed up and down the river
proved able to bear the climate. But the influence of

heathen surroundings was a far more deadly thing. Many of the Africans were true to their missionary calling and did splendid work. Others, often alone in the midst of temptation, failed under the test. The administration of the mission, as the bishop grew older, became a burden almost too heavy to be borne. Efforts made by white men to help him did not always work out well. For a time the Niger Mission passed under a cloud.

But through all Bishop Crowther was unchanged. Patient, persevering, loyal, humble in spirit, he steadily went on his way. It was said that living in an atmosphere of suspicion and of scandal, no tongue, however malicious, dared to whisper reproach against his character or his good name. Who can say how much the great Christian Church in the Niger Territories to-day owes to its first bishop? Samuel Adjai Crowther's memory is green among his own people. His story speaks, not to them only, but to all Africa and to the world.

IN UGANDA : OLD DAYS AND NEW

I. THE STORY OF MUTESA THE KING

SUNA, king of Uganda, was dead. In his reign of more than twenty years the borders of Uganda had widened.

But expansion was bought at heavy cost. Numbers of people had been killed. At home as well as abroad Suna was hated and feared. The short, close-knit man often sat silent with bent head, tracing patterns on the ground. He saw all that happened though he rarely looked up. When he fixed his eyes on any one, the executioners knew that the man was doomed and took him off to instant death. The mere announcement, " Suna is coming " sent his subjects flying out of sight. Yet this sinister man had a softer side. He was excessively fond of dogs. One special favourite did not like to eat ordinary food, so the king had a whole district planted with sweet potatoes which it preferred. When this dog died, it was buried like a human being, the body being swathed in cloth. Every chief in Uganda had to provide a bark cloth for its burial.

Suna the king was dead. He had charged the chiefs to take Kajumba, his eldest son, as their king. But Kajumba was a man of violence, and the chiefs preferred Mutesa, a younger prince, with gentle speech and large, mild eyes.

It was a goodly heritage to which the young Mutesa was called. The country had built up a life of its own. Many bad practices common among neighbouring tribes were unknown. The Baganda were the only tribe in East Africa who did not scar or mutilate their bodies, or file or remove their teeth. Sir Frederick (now Lord) Lugard, the great African administrator, wrote of these early days :

So far as we are aware, no purely pagan tribe in Africa, shut off from contact with surrounding peoples on a higher plane of civilisation, has ever developed so extraordinary a social, political, and even legal system as was found at the time of its discovery in Uganda. The first European to enter the country describes the complex system of rule ; the social organisation ; the beautiful dresses of exquisitely tanned skins or of bark cloth ; the polished manners of the people ; the high standard they had attained in their manufactures ; and the far-famed power of the king.

The royal house of Uganda traced its descent for over thirty generations, covering possibly some four hundred years. Kintu was the name of the first king. Many legends gather round him. Here is one which is found in many forms. We re-tell it from the version recorded by one of the early missionaries.[1]

A Legend of Kintu

When Kintu came to Uganda he was a great hunter. He was also a merciful man. The animals whom he caught often begged for release. " Be kind to us in the sunshine," they said, " and we will be kind to you in the rain "—that is " Help us while you are prosperous and we will help you when in need." Kintu heard them and often let his captives go free.

Kintu was not a hunter only ; he possessed great herds of cattle. One day his hunting led him far from home. When he returned all his cattle were gone. The tired hunter sought in vain for his herd. At last he met a man.

" For what, O Hunter, do you seek ? "

" For my cattle," Kintu said. " While I was absent they have gone."

" You need not look for them," replied the man ; " the gods came down from heaven and stole them all."

So Kintu went to heaven, gained entrance, and demanded that his cattle be returned. But the gods decreed that Kintu must fulfil certain tasks before he regained possession of his herd.

First, a large basket of food, enough for fifty men, was set before Kintu. He must eat it all. While he sat and contemplated his impossible task a large number of rats, whose lives he had

---

[1] *Uganda*, by Wilson and Felkin, pp. 220-1.

spared on earth, appeared and ate up the food. Kintu took the empty basket to the gods hoping to receive his herd.

But there was a second test. He was taken to a deep well without a rope, given an empty pitcher and bidden to draw water for the gods. Kintu was almost in despair; a rope he could neither make nor find. There was a rush of wings—up came a flight of swallows to whom Kintu had formerly shown mercy. They flew round the puzzled man, took the pitcher from him, winged their way down the well, and brought up the pitcher full of water. Kintu bore it joyfully to the gods.

His trial was not over yet. He was taken to an immense plain where vast herds were grazing. He was told that his cattle were there. If he picked them out without mistake he could drive them home. If he made one slip he forfeited his herd for ever. Poor Kintu! All his hopes were gone. He could not recognise his oxen among the thousands on the plain. In the midst of his perplexity a bee hummed in his ear. "I know which are your cattle. Watch me, and I will hover over them one by one." So the bee flew to and fro, and Kintu picked out his herd without mistake.

The gods restored the oxen. Kintu returned in triumph to earth.

In the stories of his ancestors Mutesa found both good examples and bad. The most that can be said for him is that he followed both. His habits did not match his gentle voice and large mild eyes. On becoming king he followed a usual custom. He killed not only his brothers, but also some of the chiefs who had placed him on the throne. He did not want any one to live who could say, " I made Mutesa king." He was afraid they would rebel against him.

To learn what Mutesa was like, and how he ruled, let us listen to three stories of the coming of white men.

The Coming of Speke

Speke was one of the travelling men who puzzled primitive Africans. Like Livingstone he was full of curiosity about rivers and lakes. He did not want to trade. He had no desire to fight or to conquer. He refused to settle down, even when land and cattle were offered him. He came into a country, and then wanted to go out again, generally in the least convenient direction. This was trying for kings and chiefs who were full of suspicion of one another.

When Speke reached Karagwe he gave Rumanika the king no peace till he was given an open way to go on to Uganda. Then he worked ceaselessly until he persuaded Mutesa to send him to Kamrasi, king of Bunyoro. He pressed Kamrasi to let him go down the Nile. The embarrassed rulers gave hundreds of reasons against his plans. But nothing would stop the determined white man. Of course Speke, and Grant who was working with him, were searching out the secrets of African geography, but Rumanika, Mutesa, and Kamrasi were hardly able to understand what this really meant.

In 1862 word was brought to Mutesa that a white man down in Karagwe sought leave to visit his court. Above all things Mutesa wanted to see a white man. His excitement knew no bounds. Slowly the long formalities were gone through. At last Speke actually arrived at the palace gates with the presents he had brought for the king.

A levee was being held in his honour. The entrance court of the palace was spacious and beautifully kept. In the second court officials of high dignity stepped forward to greet him. In the state house in the third court sat Mutesa himself. As Speke, hat in hand, advanced towards him this is what he saw :

The king, a good-looking, well-figured, tall young man of twenty-five, was sitting on a red blanket spread upon a square platform of royal grass, scrupulously well-dressed in a new bark cloth. The hair of his head was cut short, excepting on the top, where it was combed up into a high ridge. On his neck was a large ring of beautifully worked small beads. On one arm was another bead ornament, prettily devised ; on the other, a wooden charm covered with snake skin. On every finger and every toe he had alternate brass and copper rings, and above the ankle, half-way up the calf, a stocking of very pretty beads. Everything was neat, light, and elegant in its way. For a handkerchief he held a well-folded piece of bark cloth and a piece of gold embroidered silk. He took constant and copious draughts of plantain wine from neat little gourd cups, administered by his ladies-in-waiting. A white dog, spear, shield, and woman—the Uganda device—were by his side. On one hand he had a group of staff officers with whom he kept up brief conversation; on the other a band of women sorcerers.

Speke had to wait long in Uganda, partly because Grant was ill and could not join him. He became intimate with Mutesa, with the Namasole or Queen-Mother, with the Katikiro or Prime Minister, and with other officials and chiefs. Strict court rules and licence to do almost anything were strangely mixed. Mutesa had generous impulses and imperious ways. Sometimes his white guest was lavishly supplied with food. At others he was forgotten. No Baganda were allowed to take payment for food from the guests of the king. So the travellers had either to seize what they wanted from their neighbours—they had leave to do this—or to appeal to the king. " Speki," as the people called him, disliked either to steal or to beg.

Mutesa liked the company of the white man. He also liked his medicine, his rifles, and the wonderful presents he brought. But he was as impulsive as a little child. He would summon Speke to the palace, and then keep him waiting for hours in an outer court, or never see him at all that day. The king was passionately fond of shooting—it did not matter what he shot. Speke wanted him to come out after elephants or hippopotami. Mutesa found sport enough in shooting vultures sitting on a tree, or cows walking in the courtyard. Indeed, he sometimes tried his weapons on human game. One day he had a new gun and wanted to see how it worked. So he loaded it, handed it to a page and bid him go out and shoot a man. In a few moments the gun was fired and the boy came back gleefully as if he had done some amusing trick. " Did you do it well ? " asked the king.

" Capitally," replied the boy.

No one even inquired who the victim was.

Women from Mutesa's palace were lightly sent to death. When Speke moved to a residence opposite the palace gate, he saw one, two, three, or even four of the king's beautiful women led away daily to execution by the bodyguard. No one dared to respond to their cries for help.

There is a world of tragedy in one incident told by Speke. Towards the close of his stay in Uganda, he finished some business one day with the king. Not ten minutes after, he was overtaken on the road home by one of the favourite women who had given the king some unwitting offence. Instantly she was doomed to death. She was walking to execution, unbound, her hands clasped behind her head. She cried pitifully. A man walked in front, but did not touch her. She loved to give free obedience to the orders of her king. Because of her attachment to him she was allowed, as a mark of distinction, to walk unbound to her death.

When Mutesa was about, the fairest scene might be clouded by tragedy. Once he had a three-days' shooting party on the lake. They landed on an island and strolled happily among the gardens, picking what they liked. One of the king's women, young, charming, and greatly beloved, thinking to please Mutesa, offered something she had gathered to him. In a passion of rage he declared that no woman had ever dared to offer him anything for which he had not asked. He ordered the pages to seize and bind her and take her to execution. The boys slipped their cord turbans from their heads and laid hold of her. She strove to beat them off, calling on the Katikiro and on Speke for help. The other women crowded round, kneeling to the king, imploring mercy for the girl. Mutesa's fury passed all bounds. Seizing a heavy stick he began to beat the bound woman brutally on the head. The woman called "*Mzungu!*" (white man). Speke had seen the undisciplined king do many things that turned him sick. But this was too much to bear. At the risk of his life he sprang forward, seized the king's uplifted arm, and demanded that the woman be set free. The fury of the king was over in a moment. He liked novelty, and such daring interference was novel indeed. He bade the pages release the woman at once. That night he told the story to his chieftains without a shade of shame.

The Coming of Stanley

"Speki" had been gone for some twelve years when Henry M. Stanley, the man who had found Livingstone (see pp. 31, 32), came to Uganda in the course of one of his African journeys. This was in 1875. Of course, he had read Speke's *Journals* telling of Mutesa and his court. The tribes Stanley met on the way had also told of Mutesa's greatness, for his fame had gone abroad.

Mutesa prepared a great welcome for Stanley. The court was at the hunting camp on Murchison Bay. Thousands of people gathered, flags and banners waved in the breeze. Salutes were fired. The Katikiro, clad in a crimson robe over snowy white, welcomed him in Ki-Swahili. A generous present was sent to him and his men. Then he was summoned to Mutesa, who rose, came forward, and shook hands warmly. The visitor was invited to sit on an iron stool. In Speke's day this would have been an unheard-of thing. The Kabaka (king), as Stanley saw him, was a tall, clean-faced, large-eyed, nervous-looking man, spare and active. He wore a red fez and a black robe, with a white shirt belted with gold.

Stanley's knowledge of other African countries deepened his wonder at what he saw in Uganda. He admired the graceful clothing of the people. Sometimes they wore comely brown bark cloth, sometimes flowing white cotton, the use of which Mutesa had introduced among his subjects. He admired the noble canoes, bright madder brown in colour, and graceful as they rode on the grey-blue waters of the lake or went through mimic warfare. He admired the spacious neatness of the great palace, built where Mutesa could have far views over his land. He watched the king giving audience in the court and saw how Mutesa dealt with offenders and supplicants, meting out punishments and rewards. He learned something of the private parts of the palace. There Mutesa took his refreshment, or examined the treasures given him by travellers and Arab traders, or played with his female children and chatted with his favourite wives.

Traces of the cruelty of earlier days remained. Indeed things were worse than Stanley discovered, for even after he left the country Mutesa still had ears or lips cut off or eyes gouged out when he was displeased. He even killed one of the palace women with his own hand.

An incident in a naval conflict on the northern shore of the lake shows how good and bad struggled for mastery within the king. The Baganda and the Bavuma were at war. The Bavuma had just treacherously massacred Webba, a favourite page whom Mutesa sent on an embassy of peace. Shortly after a chief of the Bavuma, over sixty years of age, was taken captive by Mutesa's people. This gave opportunity for revenge. The old warrior should be publicly burnt to death. Faggots were piled high. Invitations were sent out. Stanley, who had known little Webba, was specially asked. He came, and boldly denounced the cruel purpose of the king. With burning words he protested against the deed. He reminded Mutesa of his new desires to be good. The king's fury grew ; he bid the executioners proceed. Then Stanley appealed to the ancestors of Mutesa's race as they looked down on their unworthy son. He declared that he himself would leave Uganda at once and for ever if the horrid deed were done. Mutesa suddenly melted and tears ran down his face. An hour later he sent for his friend " Stamlee," and told him the chief of the Bavuma had been forgiven.

The undoubted change in Mutesa was traced by Stanley to the influence of an Arab trader who was also a Moslem priest. He taught the king something about the religion of Islam. Mutesa found much in Islam which was better than his ancestral beliefs. For one thing, he learned to take less strong drink. Stanley soon began to talk about religion with the king. He had a Bible with him and for the first time Mutesa heard what it taught. He and his chiefs often discussed which of the two new religions was best. Stanley believed he had found in Mutesa a ready convert to Christianity. He saw in him a future apostle to Central Africa.

Fired with this idea, he wrote a letter to two leading

newspapers, one in London, another in New York, pleading
for missionaries and picturing what the future of Uganda
might be. He described the extent and the richness of the
country and the density of the population. He saw Uganda
as a field where the harvest of civilisation was ready to be
reaped. He described the kind of missionaries the " intelligent Baganda " needed. They were not to be only
preachers, but men who could teach how to live the Christian
life, who could cure diseases, and knew how to improve
agriculture and the building of houses. He declared that
Mutesa was ready to welcome missionaries and to support
their work. " The people on the shores of the Nyanza call
upon you," he wrote. " I assure you that in one year you
will have more converts to Christianity than all other
missions can number."

The letter was entrusted to a Belgian officer, Linant de
Bellefonds, who came into Uganda from the Sudan. Being
a French Protestant, like the missionaries who went to
Moshoeshoe (see p. 18), he helped Stanley to teach the
king. On his way back to Egypt, Linant de Bellefonds
was murdered by the Bari tribe. He had hidden Stanley's
letter in his long riding boot. A party of soldiers were sent
out to punish the Bari. De Bellefonds' body was recovered ;
the blood-stained letter was found in the boot. It was sent
to General Gordon at Khartum, who forwarded it to its
destination.

That letter played a great part in the future destinies of
Uganda. The heart of England was stirred by Stanley's
appeal. Money was quickly given. Men offered for the
work. Within two years white missionaries were in Karagwe
on their way to Mutesa the king.

The Coming of the Missionaries

They waited, of course, for permission to enter Uganda.
As soon as this reached them, two pioneer missionaries
crossed the lake to Entebbe. They made their way to
Rubaga, then the capital of Mutesa's kingdom, in 1877.
Within the next few years others came in groups, some

entered from the south, others by the Nile route which
reaches Uganda from the north. The earliest missionaries
were English, belonging to the Anglican Church. In 1879
two French Roman Catholic priests were sent by Cardinal
Lavigerie. They asked for permission to settle in Uganda
and were admitted by the king. Thus began the two
missions which have transformed the life of the land.

Among the early British missionaries was Alexander
Mackay, the fearless Scottish engineer. Ashe, another man
who came later, wrote a vivid description [1] of the scene when
he went with a companion to see Mutesa. Let us walk
beside the newcomer as he soberly rides on his donkey and
see things through his eyes.

Approaching the King

Mutesa's *lubiri* looks like a great village of gigantic straw
houses in beehive shape. From it flashes a little panting page,
wearing the *luga* or necklet of bent cane which marks him as
serving the Kabaka. He calls in Luganda " Come ! Come ! "
After him comes another little fellow crying " Be quick ! "

A wide gateway opens into a spacious court surrounded by
the royal fence of reeds. It is a bright and busy scene. Here is
the gigantic figure of the Kabaka's chief herdsman, followed by a
skin-clad company ; there is a group of musicians from Busoga,
dancing as they pass. Here come some potters bearing on their
heads enormous earthenware vessels, their tribute to the king.
See that great chief—Mukwenda of Singo—clad in a scarlet coat
of fine cloth richly embroidered in gold. In his hand is a long,
highly polished, white staff, on his head a red fez. He stalks
along like an emperor, yet a few years ago he was a drummer
boy. Following him come a crowd of his vassals, a wee slave
boy bearing his pipe and shoes, another slave carrying his graceful
little drinking gourd, its long bent tube exquisitely plaited with
fine coloured grass.

We have reached the entrance to the third court. Ashe
dismounts from his donkey. Here comes a splendid looking man,
blazing in crimson and gold. Is he Mutesa ? No, only the
keeper of the palace. On through another gateway ; the

---

[1] *Two Kings of Uganda*, by R. P. Ashe. The book is now out of print·
Pages 48 to 62 are summarised here.

Katikiro comes to meet his guests. This small, handsome, suave, treacherous, far-seeing man is one of the long succession of Prime Ministers which continues still. Travellers call him the Bismarck of Uganda. He is said to rule even the king.

The summons to Mutesa's presence has not yet been given. Watch the Katikiro as he goes on with his work. He sits judging cases. There is before him a *mweso* board. All the time his lithe fingers gather up the counters and drop them in their proper holes. Then he stops his game ; the case has been concluded ; the judgment has to be given. He arranges some small white sticks on the ground before him, in the order of the statement he is going to make. Then he speaks.

The deep-toned royal drums are heard in a rolling tattoo. There is a blare of trumpets. The call to the king's levee has come. The Katikiro rises ; his court is deserted in a moment. He and the other chiefs enter the precincts of the great court followed by the two white men. Jostling them are scarlet-coated Baganda noblemen, chiefs from Busoga and elsewhere, representatives of the Bahuma lords, Arabs from Muscat, run-away Egyptian soldiers from the Sudan, adventurers from the East Coast and Madagascar, mountebanks, minstrels, dancers, and dwarfs.

The wide doorway of the reception- house is reached. Mutesa lies on a low couch under a canopy of bark cloth, clothed from head to foot in a snowy robe. In his hand is a small looking-glass. Two handsome boys stand at the foot of his couch. One warms his master's feet, the other brushes away flies. Chiefs are grouped near the king. The women of the household are behind. A camp stool is provided for Ashe. His appearance is examined and commented on. Certain business is transacted between the king and his chiefs. Then Mutesa waves his hand and the assembly is dismissed.

Mutesa's Place in History

It is not easy to estimate justly the character of this remarkable man. In his early days he was fickle, passionate and without self-control. Mutesa, as Speke knew him, had few of the qualities of a king. His early love of sport seemed to grow into something more manly. In his *History of the Kings of Uganda* Sir Apolo Kagwa writes of him as a great sportsman, who surpassed all his chiefs in strength.

He called up the strongest men from the provinces and set them to fight with sticks. It was a rough game in which men were sometimes killed. But it called out the courage of the boldest. Mutesa also arranged great wrestling matches in which prizes were given. He was a fine swimmer and enjoyed all water sports. He had a small lake made for these near his court.

The cruelty and brutality which his forefathers practised clung to him to the end of his days. He was known to his people as Mukabya, the Tear Maker. He is held, nevertheless, to have been the greatest of all the kings of Uganda. He was able and ambitious. Contact with the wider world enlarged his mind. He was generally courteous to white men. His outlook on life grew less sordid ; he grew more disciplined in his ways. He encouraged trade, especially across the lake. He sent two envoys to England accompanied by a missionary. They were the first two delegates sent from Central Africa. But he showed how little he understood life by secretly choosing two slaves to go instead of chiefs. During his reign the customs of the country and the dress of the people changed. The national bark cloth began to give place to cotton, hitherto only allowed to be worn by chiefs.

Mutesa reordered the army and himself directed war. He had a large board with holes and pegs on which he marked where his soldiers were. A red peg meant a thousand men, a black peg one hundred, a white peg ten. When he wished to send out a military expedition he pulled out a certain number of pegs and handed them to a chief. He had no more trouble : the thing was done.

The first people who influenced Mutesa were Moslem traders, from whom he learned how to read and write ; he could speak Arabic and Ki-Swahili. Then he came under the influence of Christian missionaries from overseas. He gave land for mission purposes. He listened to the Christian message, but he never laid hold of it for himself. The quick Baganda learned to read and write. As fast as books were printed they were eagerly bought. Many belonging to the court came to be prepared for baptism. Among them

" young Kagwa " is named. Stanley's prophecy of what would happen if missionaries came to Uganda began to be fulfilled. But Mutesa was not the leader of the movement, as Stanley had hoped.

Mutesa fell into bad health and suffered greatly. As he grew worse the weary expression on his face was pitiful to behold. Arab traders, who professed to have curative medicines, tried their powers in vain. The missionaries did for him all that they could. At last he withdrew into the recesses of his palace and no one knows the details of his closing days.

In October, 1884, it was made known to the country that Mutesa, in many ways a great and worthy descendant of Kintu, was gathered to his fathers. Mwanga his son reigned in his stead. By his own orders the jawbone of the king was not removed for separate burial, nor was his body embalmed. Many ancient customs connected with royal funerals were not observed. But the whole country —especially the peasants, who passionately revered him— mourned for the dead king. The men wore bark cloth girded with withered plantain fibre. The women wore girdles of tattered green plantain leaves.

II. SIR APOLO KAGWA, K.C.M.G., M.B.E.

An Eventful Span of Life

Sir Apolo Kagwa, Katikiro (Prime Minister) of Uganda, died at Nairobi in February, 1927. He belonged to the ancient Nsenene (grasshopper) clan. His grandfather, Bunya, was the county chief of Bulemezi ; he was called the Kangao.

Prime ministers in western lands have seen changes in the fortunes of their countries. But few have seen such sweeping changes as took place in Kagwa's country in his lifetime. Those sixty-two years cover almost the whole span of the white man's contact with Uganda. Three years after Speke visited the country Kagwa was born.

Two years after Stanley's visit he became a page at Mutesa's court.   He was a favourite pupil of the first missionaries.

When Kagwa was born not a boy or girl in all Uganda was in school.   Uganda had no written language of its own.   Useful lessons were learned by boys and girls from the folk-lore and ancient legends told by old men and women.   The life of the tribe was full of discipline, some of it wholesome and good, some of it holding a great deal that was superstitious, hurtful, and cruel.   Boys and girls had no chance of learning more than their fathers knew.

When Kagwa died, Uganda was covered with a network of schools.   Thousands of little bush schools in remote districts led up to the new Government College at Makerere. There were day schools and boarding schools, both for boys and girls.   There were schools for training teachers and schoolmasters and clergymen.   Boys were being taught trades and agriculture.   Girls were being trained not only as teachers and schoolmistresses but for all the duties of motherhood and the home.   There were thousands of pupils in the Uganda schools.   Highly educated Baganda were serving their country.   Some, like Kagwa himself, were guiding and administrating Native affairs.   Others were clergy, teachers, schoolmasters, schoolmistresses, nurses, hospital assistants, or office helpers.   Many through education had become skilful carpenters and builders, better road-makers and bridge-builders.

When Kagwa was born it took months of toilsome marching to reach the Victoria Nyanza from the coast, and many days to cross the lake in canoes.   When Kagwa died, the train from Mombasa took two days to its terminus on the north-eastern shore of the lake.   Thence twenty-two hours in a good steamboat brought the traveller to Uganda. Further railways were under constructon ; motors traversed the land ; the sound of aeroplanes could be heard.   Trade in his boyhood was small, except in slaves and ivory.   When he died the exports of Uganda were quoted in the markets of the world.   Wealth, especially from the sales of cotton, was transforming Baganda life.

When Kagwa was born there was little knowledge of

how to care for the sick.   The ancient use of herbal remedies
was mixed up with sorcery and superstition.   The treatment was often worse than the disease.   Witch doctors
used their incantations as the servants of hatred, jealousy,
and revenge.   Poison ordeals were common.   There was
no preventive medicine, no teaching of hygiene.   Surgery
was practised by those who had no knowledge of the human
frame.   Babies died off like flies and broke the hearts of
their mothers.   Women suffered horribly during and after
child-birth for lack of proper treatment and care.   When
Kagwa died, the Government were spending £120,000 a
year on medical service and the missions were busily at
work.   First-class hospitals were filled with patients.
Major operations were being successfully performed in up-
to-date theatres.   Training in hospital work and midwifery
was being given to Baganda men and women.   Child
welfare centres were established.   In the desperate battle
against sleeping sickness, science and devotion had won.

When Kagwa was born, there was in Uganda and the
surrounding districts no group of Christians, possibly no
single Christian of African race.   When he died, a great
Christian community attached to the two missions covered
the land.   Most of the leading chiefs were Christian ; in
the National Council (*Lukiko*) only eight Moslems and one
pagan were to be found.   The two missions were responsible
for nearly all the schools.   The Synod which governed the
Native Anglican Church was mainly African in membership ;
there were some sixty ordained Baganda clergy, and two
Baganda canons attached to the cathedral.   All through
the country important work in Church and school was
under African leadership.   Uganda had even sent out its
own sons and daughters as missionaries to tribes of other
languages far away, and was supporting them and their
work.

In the changes and developments of this eventful span
of sixty years, no African played a larger part than did
Apolo Kagwa himself.   He stood at the heart of his
country's life, a steady influence for advance.

From Mwanga to Daudi Chwa

The pitiful story of Mwanga's reign, in succession to that of Mutesa his father, cannot be told here. If men of force and character like Apolo Kagwa had not stood by Uganda, the rising sun of prosperity would have set. Such honour as came to Mwanga was given to his position as king. As a man it was not easy for his people to give him either love or respect.

At first Mwanga showed interest in the two religions which were taking root in his land—Islam and Christianity. After a time he turned against them both. He began to persecute the Christians as fiercely as Nero did at Rome. Kagwa and a companion page lifted up their voices in protest and confessed their faith. One lad was flung to the executioners, the other—Kagwa—was too valuable to be killed. But Mwanga laid his head open with a terrible spear wound which left a life-long scar. At least two hundred Christians, many of them lads just entering life, were massacred by order of the king. The whole world was stirred by the heroism of the martyrs of Uganda as they faced fire and sword. It was Mwanga who sent orders to Luba to murder Bishop Hannington in Busoga, because contrary to custom he had approached Uganda from the eastern side. It was Kagwa who brought the missionaries the direful news. Those were dark days in Uganda for the little band of white men and for their friends.

As the days passed Kagwa's influence grew. His great stature and imposing presence fitted him to be bearer to the king. On state occasions, according to the old Uganda custom, he bore Mwanga shoulder high. He became the royal storekeeper, a position of responsibility and trust. In the wars which succeeded one another in Mwanga's unhappy reign he proved himself a brave and resourceful warrior. He became the leading general of the armies. Mwanga made him Katikiro in 1889.

The ship of state was not easy to steer in Mwanga's day. The channel to be passed through was rocky ; currents

were conflicting ; tides ran high. Within the country three
parties were in opposition to one another, sometimes even
at war. The followers of the French mission (see p. 87),
now known as the Bafransa, had grown strong. So had
the followers of the English mission, the Bangreza. The
Mohammedan party, backed by Kabarega, king of Bunyoro,
and reinforced by some Sudanese soldiers, sought to gain
control of affairs. It was a conflict of political rather than
of religious interests.

Confusion was increased by the European influences now
pushing their way into Uganda. Representatives of the
Imperial British East Africa Company came desiring a
treaty for trade. Mwanga accepted their flag. Representatives of Germany came offering a treaty. This Mwanga
readily signed. Difficult questions began to be asked about
the relation of Uganda to Germany and to England. But
in 1890 it was agreed in an Anglo-German Treaty that
Uganda lay in the British sphere of influence. The Company
carried on administration and work in the country till the
British flag was unfurled at Kampala in April, 1893 ; the
Protectorate was voted in the House of Commons in London
in June, 1894.

Mwanga and his Prime Minister stand out in striking
contrast in these troublous days. Mwanga was timid and
blustering in turn. He tried to make use first of one party,
then of another. He ended by being forsaken of all. He
fled from his kingdom ; he was forgiven and recalled ; then
he led a revolt against those who had befriended him.
Finally, the weak and vicious king forfeited the last confidence of his own people and of the British officials. He
was deposed in 1899 and deported to the Seychelles Islands.
There Mwanga was taught by a Baganda teacher. He
became a Christian and was baptised. He died in 1903.
In 1910 his body was brought to Uganda for burial. It
was taken with great ceremony from the cathedral to
Mutesa's grave, where father and son now lie side by side.

Apolo Kagwa, on the contrary, rose to the needs of the
time. He was loyal, where loyalty was possible, to his
degenerate king. But loyalty to the interests of his country

came first. He played a wise patriot's part. Uganda was divided into three parties, Kagwa did not attempt to hide his opinion as to which was in the right. He belonged to the Bangreza, but he wanted liberty and fair play for all. During the difficult days when Captain (afterwards Lord) Lugard was acting for the Imperial British East Africa Company, Apolo Kagwa stood by his side and helped. When the Company withdrew and the British Protectorate was established, Kagwa encouraged the Kabaka and the people to accept the new plans. But he was watchful of the interests of his country. He did not approve plans until he was sure how they would work out. He was reasonable and independent in his judgment, so his opinion carried weight.

Mwanga's infant son, born in 1896, was proclaimed Kabaka of Uganda in 1897, under the title of Daudi Chwa. Three regents were appointed for his minority, of whom Apolo Kagwa was one. With courage, ability, and devotion he added the duties of regent to those of Katikiro. He bent all his energies to the service of his little master. He was a skilful leader in adjusting national life to the new day which had dawned.

A few years later Kagwa stepped out into the wider world. King Edward VII, successor to Queen Victoria, was to be crowned in London in 1902. Uganda, now within the British Empire, must be represented at so great an event. In the childhood of King Daudi, the choice of Apolo Kagwa as delegate was best. The months which the Katikiro spent in England were rich in good fellowship. He met and made friends with many famous men. He visited centres of industry. He gleaned for his country experience of many kinds. His splendid physique, his quiet dignity, and his quick intelligence were a revelation of what an African could be. The King received him at Buckingham Palace. He was present at the coronation in Westminster Abbey. After his return to Africa he was made a Knight Commander of St. Michael and St. George, one of the first Africans to receive the honour of the K.C.M.G.

Ham Mukasa, the chief who accompanied him as

secretary, wrote a large book about their tour. It was written first in Luganda and then translated into English. Many people in both countries read it still.

HOW THE NEW DAY TOOK SHAPE

There has been no more thrilling adventure in modern African history than that of shaping the new day in Uganda. The uncertain rule of Mwanga was over. The British Protectorate had been established on lines which left scope for the development of national life. The people were intelligent and eager to be taught. What was good in the old day had prepared the way for what was good in the new. There was no reason why the time-honoured system of the past should conflict with the new administration. It was possible to adjust the one to the other. And the right men for the task were on the spot. Sir Apolo Kagwa, though he stood foremost, did not stand alone. There were other chiefs like-minded. Co-operation between British officials and African leaders began in mutual respect.

In 1899 a special Commissioner—Sir H. H. Johnston— was sent out from England to make inquiry and confer with those on the spot. As a result the Uganda Agreement, dealing with questions of land, of law, and of taxation, was drawn up in 1900. Some of its provisions have needed to be adjusted, but it remains the charter of the new day in Uganda still. Until his death in the summer of 1927 Sir H. H. Johnston watched the old stream of Uganda life flowing in the new channels he had cut, and he was glad.

How is the work of administration carried on in Uganda to-day ? Let us put our question to that Chief who has just been to see his son, a young student at Makerere, and is about to return to his country house in his motor-car. He has a big stake in the near future of Uganda because of his promising boy, and has a heritage stretching through a long line of chiefs into the past. Let us ask him tell to us how the work of his country is carried on.

He will explain that, now as for centuries, Uganda is divided into a number of districts, each under chiefs.

To-day there are twenty *saza* or counties ; each of these is divided into several *gombolola* or districts. There are numbers of sub-districts as well. Each territory, whether large or small, has a special title for its chief, and the chiefs and sub-chiefs take rank in a special order. At the head of all the chiefs is the Kabaka or king. He has three special ministers to help him to rule. These are the Katikiro or Prime Minister, the Native Chief Justice, and the Treasurer. The Kabaka is no longer an absolute monarch, as Mutesa and Mwanga were. But he is known as the Native Ruler of the kingdom of Buganda,[1] called the province of Buganda under the protection and over-rule of Great Britain. He has the title of " His Highness " from the British Government.

The Kabaka exercises direct rule over his people through the *Lukiko* or National Council. It is one of the most interesting parliaments in the world. Our friend from Makerere is a member of it and can tell us how it works. The *Lukiko* has some ninety members, including the three ministers who assist the king. The Katikiro, or one of the other two, presides. The chief of each *saza* has a seat ; if he cannot attend he can send a representative. Three notable persons from each *saza*, and six additional men of importance nominated by the Kabaka, are also members. The *Lukiko* has power to discuss all matters concerning Native administration. Resolutions carried by a majority are sent on to the Kabaka. The sanction of the British authorities is required to give them effect. Our informant, with his knowledge of local history, will tell us that the power of the *Lukiko* is growing, and that he wants his boy to be a member one day. British officials are seeking to build up the influence of the National Council and to utilise its work.

But what about justice throughout the country ? Can the Chief tell us how Law Courts work to-day ? Have they forsaken the ways of old Uganda ? Are they set up on Western lines ? Not at all. There are still the courts of

---

[1] Uganda now stands for the whole Protectorate ; Buganda is the term officially used for the kingdom or province.

the sub-chiefs, which have defined civil and criminal jurisdiction in their area. In them first-grade sub-chiefs, aided by other sub-chiefs and elders of the district, preside. If these courts cannot deal with any question, or if their action needs to be revised, there is a court for each county, presided over by the *saza* chief and his assessors. These courts have fuller civil and criminal powers. Once more, above these there is the court composed of seven members of the *Lukiko*, over which the Kabaka or one of the three ministers presides. It has full jurisdiction, civil and criminal, in all cases where both parties are Baganda. It can revise the work of its own subordinate courts. On certain subjects the British Courts supervise its work, and to them come cases involving the death penalty. All this, the Chief will tell us, is no mere paper scheme. •

Truly Sir Apolo Kagwa, in promoting union between the best in Uganda and the best in Great Britain, has left a wide prospect of service and of partnership open to Baganda youth. The students at Makerere will not lack for spheres of work.

Social Service and Church Work

Sir Apolo served his country in many different ways. He loved the old legends and customs of his people. He wanted the younger men and women to know what their ancestors had done and thought. He wrote two books about old Uganda. One is called the *History of the Kings of Uganda* ; the other is *Uganda Folk-lore*. Both works are in Luganda, not in English. One of the missionaries in Uganda, named Roscoe, studied all these things. His books on ancient customs and legends and religion are in the great libraries in America and Europe where people go to study, and where new books are prepared. Sir Apolo helped to collect information for this English missionary scholar.

The Katikiro knew where men and women who remembered the old days were to be found. He used to gather these people into his house that they might tell the

English scholar what their fathers did. He got priests and diviners from all the old temples ; he found representatives of all the different clans. Some of the old people lived a hundred miles away. But Sir Apolo had them comfortably carried to his house, and kept them as his guests while they answered questions and told their ancient tales. In one of the English scholar's books there is a fine plan of the old capital of Uganda drawn by the Katikiro himself, and a map of the royal enclosure where the kings once lived. In the preface the author thanks his friend Sir Apolo Kagwa for all the help he gave.

The curse of slavery ate deeply into Uganda life. The chiefs held large numbers of slaves, and constantly added to them the prisoners taken in local wars. Worse still, under the influence of Arabs from the coast an extensive trade in slaves sprang up. Mackay used to say that Mutesa was the worse slave-hunter in the world. Before the British flag was hoisted in Uganda the conscience of the Christians was troubled about these slaves. Was it right that human beings should be held in bondage, to be bought and sold like cattle or fowls ?

The Christians took counsel with Bishop Tucker. He pointed them to the Bible, which teaches the Christian way of life. The slave-owning Christians read what was written, and prayed for light. Light came. But it is often easier to see a duty than to do it. They saw that the slaves should be released, though it meant a heavy loss of property, especially for the larger chiefs. The Christians made up their minds to do right. Forty of the leading chiefs drew up a declaration, signed it, and brought it to the Bishop. It contained these words : " We hereby agree to untie and free completely all our slaves." The first name signed to the paper was that of the Katikiro.

We have seen Sir Apolo serving his country in the troublous days of Mwanga's reign. He administered affairs with equal skill and judgment as regent for Mwanga's infant son. When Kabaka Daudi Chwa came of age in 1914, Sir Apolo ceased to be regent, but retained his office as Prime Minister until 1926—a period of thirty-five years.

During the Great War (1914–1918) he and the Kabaka co-operated with the British officials in the protection of the frontier between Uganda and German territory. Sir Apolo, who had welcomed the British to Uganda, was ready to see all the resources of the country used on the Allies' behalf.

The Katikiro was always a leader in educational and social advance. Though no school was available for him in his boyhood, he secured good education for his sons, first in Uganda, then in England. He pressed the importance of education upon the people. He started primary schools in many outlying districts himself. He backed the missionaries in plans for new educational work, and was a member of the Board of Education for the diocese. Missionaries constantly tell of his generous contributions to school funds ; or of his special gifts, such as a four-faced striking clock to one institution ; or of his close personal interest in individual boys and girls. They tell of his keen interest in schools for girls, of his belief that they, too, must receive higher education. The great Mission Hospital at Mengo has stories to tell of his friendly aid. He visited the wards every Sunday on his way home from the cathedral service. He chatted with each patient and never seemed to hurry.

He led the way in the improvement of houses and in sanitation. He believed in industrial work, and sometimes himself helped to teach bricklaying or carpentry. He introduced typewriters, which have now become common in the offices of the chiefs. He furthered the cotton industry by distributing thousands of better plants and helping the people to improve methods of cultivation. He got out a small printing press from England and issued little papers full of useful information for farmers in rural areas.

The Native Anglican Church in Uganda will always associate the building and rebuilding of the Great Cathedral on Namirembe Hill with the Katikiro. Here is the story of his share in the work.

Cathedral and Katikiro

For the third time in the short history of Christianity in Uganda the Cathedral Church on Namirembe needed to be rebuilt. The perishable materials only lasted six or seven years. Timber, reeds, and grass made a structure beautiful to look on. In the great aisles there were golden and brown lights and shadows which were an artist's joy. But the Christians could not keep on always rebuilding their Cathedral. Could not some more permanent building be raised ?

In 1901 plans for a new Cathedral were agreed on. It was to be built of brick, the roof being thatched and lined with polished reeds. The Katikiro called a meeting of leading Christians. The cost of the building was calculated and divided up into shares. Those present stated how much they could give. The regents gave most ; the lesser chiefs gave in proportion. Then the whole body of Church members set to work.

" It was an inspiring sight," says Bishop Tucker, " to see long strings of men going to the swamps day by day to dig clay, and then to see them wend their way up the steep hillside of Namirembe with heavy loads of clay upon their heads." The procession was often led by the Katikiro himself, bearing with his great strength a load heavier than the rest. Women went into the forests to gather wood for burning the bricks for the foundations. Princesses and wives of chiefs vied with peasant women in the work. The foundation stone was laid by King Daudi Chwa. The Cathedral was finished and consecrated in 1904.

But alas ! in 1910 lightning struck the building. The thatched roof blazed. The place was destroyed in an hour. The patient people set to work again. This time not even the roof should be of reeds. A few Europeans and a larger group of Baganda formed a Building Committee. The Katikiro took the lead ; one of the missionaries was Secretary to the Committee.

It is a splendid story of self-sacrificing effort, carried on through the strain of the Great War. Without the inspiring leadership of Sir Apolo the needed money could not have been raised. The chiefs agreed to give 30 per cent. of their income from land. For years the Katikiro regularly collected this. He added 30 per cent. of his own rentals and sent the whole amount, with full details, to the Treasurer of the Building Fund. The giving of poor as well as of rich was wonderful. In a country where the workman's daily wage was about fourpence the Baganda paid in £18,000. At last the beautiful building with its tiled roof was completed. It was consecrated in September, 1919. In it the great celebrations of the jubilee of the Uganda Mission centred in June, 1927.

Sir Apolo Kagwa at Home

The Katikiro built himself a very fine house on his return from England, with modern fittings, such as electric bells. Here he loved to entertain his friends. Wedding receptions were common on Saturday afternoons. Prize givings, too, he liked, especially for the Mengo Boys' High School. On Thursdays there was a Chiefs' Bible Class, held when the meeting of the *Lukiko* closed. As many as seventy sometimes came. One of the missionaries spoke.

When distinguished visitors came to Uganda the Katikiro often gave an afternoon party in their honour. Since the Kabaka came of age, the official gatherings are held at his house. We have been with one missionary to the court of Mutesa. Let us go with another to a party at Sir Apolo Kagwa's house.

An Afternoon Party

Here is the invitation, printed at Kampala, in gold on a white card :

> ### Sir Apolo Kagwa
> requests the pleasure of the company of
> . . . .
> on . . . . . . at four o'clock to meet
> (*Here the distinguished visitor is named*).
> R.S.V.P.

The last four letters stand for a French sentence—" Respondez, s'il vous plait." That means—" Please reply." Sir Apolo has copied just what is done by his English friends.

There stands the large two-storied house, close to the Kabaka's. It can be seen for miles round. The gatekeeper

SIR APOLO KAGWA AND HIS WIFE.
Photo by Alfred Lobo, Kampala.

puts both his hands together and bows in welcome as we drive through the open gates. Note the huge keys hanging from his waist.

We draw up by the wide steps leading to the front door. Ah! there is the lovely view of the Cathedral. Out of a group of attendants one comes forward in Native dress. He ushers us through the hall to the reception-room. Here another man goes before us into the room, kneels before the Katikiro and tells him we have come.

The great Prime Minister towers above the rest. His appearance is formidable, his expression rather severe. But his roving eyes rest on us; he crosses the room in hurried movements, both hands outstretched. The sternness has gone from his face. He is glad to see us, without a doubt. He is wearing a European coat over his white *kanzu*. If this were an official reception he would be in his splendid robes.

We are given seats. Here come the lesser chiefs one by one to greet us and say they are glad we have come. We are early, so we watch the guests arrive, on foot, or on bicycles, or in motor cars. There are many Europeans—some Government officials, a few business men and their wives, missionaries, and one or two people from Entebbe, the town down on the lake. There are no Baganda ladies. Samali, Sir Apolo's wife, is the friend of many. But she belongs to the older school and does not receive guests with her husband, as the Kabaka's young wife would do.

Here comes the tea, on trays borne by Native servants. Sir Apolo likes to entertain English friends in their own fashion, so there is bread and jam and iced cake. Look round and notice on the walls the enlarged photographs of groups and the personal photographs on the Katikiro's writing table. There is a gramophone, too. The settees, armchairs, camp chairs, and the carpeted floor are unlike old Uganda, and the windows have mosquito nets. There, at the end of the room, is a fine grandfather's clock, with a brass tablet showing that it was presented to the Katikiro as a token of regard by the Acting Governor.

It is time to go. We came early; the bicycles and cars of departing guests are already passing down by the lawn, with its orange trees, and out through the open gates. As we leave, we write our name in the Katikiro's guest book. See how many pages the names of his visitors fill.

Kagwa's True Eminence

We have traced this great man's career from boyhood to maturity, from the responsibilities of public life into the privacy of his home. Neither in private nor in public was he faultless. But he stands out as an eminent African who rendered noble service to his country and who was generous and unchanging to his many friends. His patriotism and ability have won for him lasting fame. In a fine appreciation which appeared in the London *Morning Post* immediately after his death, written by the *aide-de-camp* of a former governor, full justice was done to his share in shaping Uganda's new day.

To be Prime Minister of so progressive a country as Uganda is no light task. To rule over an enlightened Native Parliament calls for qualities and brains of no mean order. He framed rules and procedures which enable his countrymen to take a hand at governing themselves . . . to dispense laws and justice to their own people, in their own Parliament, with their own Cabinet.

Nor does this testimony stand alone. From other leading English papers the following sentences are taken.

His race may claim that entering the world of written history but yesterday it has already produced a statesman.

He took a leading part in building the present-day Uganda. He was a Native statesman, administrator and general, now helping to govern his country peacefully, now leading an army.

Kagwa was intimately associated in constructive effort with a succession of British administrators.

He enjoyed the confidence of successive governors and had a deserved reputation as a statesman.

JOHN TENGO JABAVU, EDITOR AND PATRIOT [1]

How the Boy Grew Up

IN the middle of the nineteenth century a man of the Fingoes lived in Healdtown, about nine miles from Fort Beaufort in Cape Province. Ntwanambi was his name. He was a labourer, working for builders or on the roads. His grandson describes him as a man with a majestic forehead, large ears, flashing eyes, and big hands and feet. He was tall and jet black. He was a famous walker who could tramp from Healdtown to Grahamstown and back.

Mary Mpinde, his wife, was a handsome little woman, a good singer, and a vigorous ruler at home. She was a washerwoman, and earned a little extra money by selling tin dishes of grain to the local grocery store. She and her husband belonged to the Wesleyan Mission at Healdtown. Their first son, John Tengo Jabavu, was born in January, 1859. His mother set herself to save money to pay for his schooling. The sturdy, resolute little woman lived to see three daughters and two sons doing well in life.

At ten years of age Tengo began to earn his daily bread. Clad in one little shirt he herded cattle among the hills. Before long he was sent to school, but he herded cattle still. The moment class was over he hastened to his work, taking his midday meal to eat among his beasts. Tengo wanted to excel in class. But he could not do home work like the other boys, for his parents had neither a table nor

[1] Most of the material for this story has been taken from *The Life of John Tengo Jabavu, A Great Bantu Patriot*, by D. D. T. Jabavu, B.A. (London). Published at the Lovedale Institution Press, C.P.

a lamp. So the boy learned to depend on his memory. This helped him in after life. He did well in school. As a reward his uncle gave him a red jacket. This was Tengo's first success in life.

The boy's whole heart was in his studies. In Healdtown there was a fine teacher. He set the door of knowledge open and his pupils entered in. Tengo overtook most of his companions; then he began to leave some of them behind. He gave every spare moment to his tasks. Yet he was a merry boy and full of mischief. He loved to play practical jokes both on teacher and on boys; he even ventured to do this in class. The School Committee wanted to expel him, but the wise teacher said that mischief was not always evil. So Tengo stayed on.

The Healdtown boys were very independent in their ways. The afternoon manual labour class cultivated the fruit garden. They grew fine fruit, but season after season they were not given any of it to eat. They agreed to pocket some for their own use. Their misdeeds were soon detected. Tengo, who had been one of the leaders, was brought before the master. He reasoned the case, showing that the sense of injustice was strong among the boys. Then he quoted the text, " Who planteth a vineyard and eateth not the fruit thereof ? " The master admitted the injustice. The culprits were forgiven. Henceforth the boys had due share of the fruit.

Tengo, like many boys, loved long words, whether in English or in Xosa. One of the senior students used to ask him constantly in English how he was. Tengo got tired of this. He waited till the question was asked on a day when a group of boys stood round. Then he gravely replied, " I am still in good salubrity, although there are symptoms which symbolise morbosity." His tormentor was well laughed at and asked him questions no more.

At last Tengo had gone right up the school; the time for the final examination came. It was one for which a fee had to be paid. Ntwanambi and Mary Mpinde had not the money. But one of their two ploughing oxen, named Falteyn, was sold and the fee was paid. Tengo left school with his teacher's certificate. His mother's dream was coming to pass.

Tengo was now seventeen. He got a post in a school at Somerset East, where he had to live in a poor neighbourhood. On Saturdays the streets were full of dancing and low music. Drunkenness was rife. But Tengo kept out of the way of temptation and worked hard. His pupils learned to love study because their young teacher did. He made friends with the parents of the children. He shared in the life and work of the Church. He tried to help all plans for the social welfare of Somerset East.

The Budding Editor

In later days Tengo Jabavu was described as " a born editor." He certainly had the love of journalism in his blood. At Somerset East he apprenticed himself to a printer's office. He began work there at four o'clock each morning. After breakfast he went to his day's teaching. In the evenings he studied with a good tutor and made rapid progress in Greek and Latin. How he pored over the newspapers which came to the printer's office ! He wanted to know what men were doing, what they thought. The world of politics enthralled him. Presently he began to write himself. He made friends with the distinguished editor of the *Cape Argus*. He was asked to write for it papers on local news. He did not sign these articles, but people noticed that they were very good.

In 1881 a new door opened. He was invited to go to Lovedale Institution to edit their paper *Isigidimi Sama Xosa* (the *Xosa Express*) for three years. At Lovedale, under its great Scottish principal, James Stewart, Jabavu spent the happiest years of his life. While he edited he threw himself into the life of the great institution. He seized the educational chances which came his way. The literary society was active ; he took brilliant part in its debates. There were splendid books in the library ; he read them one by one. He passed the matriculation examination of the South African University in 1883. Only one African had done this before.

All the time he studied the Cape Town parliamentary debates. He observed how the machinery of government worked. He formed a high ideal of the duties of political life. He saw what good laws could do. He began to go to meetings himself as a speaker on political questions. This did not quite fit in with his Lovedale work. His agreement as editor ended in 1884.

Jabavu now wished to marry and have a home of his own. He chose a bride, but his mother did not approve. Then she made a selection which happily pleased her son. Elda Sakuba was a minister's daughter. Like Mary Mpinde she sang well. She visited Lovedale with a mixed choir whose singing took the place by storm. She and young Jabavu had a true-love courtship. They were married early in 1885.

What next? Teaching or journalism? The young man longed to be an independent Native journalist. A periodical to speak for the Bantu people was needed. But it cost money to start a paper and Jabavu had no capital. And now he was setting up a home. Just at the critical moment there came in sight another open door. Jabavu went right through.

A general election was approaching. Some Dutch and Native voters wanted Mr. Jabavu to stand for Victoria East. But he had studied the political situation. He knew that a good white member could do more for the Native cause. The right person was at hand in the future Chief Justice of the Union of South Africa, Mr. James Rose-Innes. So Jabavu became the principal Native supporter of the Rose-Innes party. He refused to take any payment for his work.

By the time the election was over he had proved his worth. He showed knowledge of political affairs. He grasped the meaning of the situation. He spoke well both in Xosa and in English. He had clear convictions which he was not afraid to express. It was admitted that he had materially helped to win the seat. But the persistent question as to his future work remained. What next ?

Then a brother of the newly elected member, with a friend, offered to guarantee the expenses if Mr. Jabavu would edit an independent Native paper. They would back his credit at the Bank. It was one of those generous offers which release a man for life. Jabavu had got his chance. All his plans and dreams took shape in action. At twenty-four years of age he found himself founder, proprietor, and editor of *Imvo Zabantsundu* (*Native Opinion*), the first journal devoted to Native interests and expressing Native views in South Africa. He loved every bit of the journal and its work. It was for this he had toiled from four o'clock in the morning at Somerset East. He shouldered his new undertaking without a moment's delay. He was his own clerk. He was advertising agent for the paper, travelling far into the country to secure subscribers. He read all his own proofs. He is said to have written over 2,000 leading articles for *Imvo* in English and in Xosa.

How thankful Ntwanambi and Mary Mpinde must have been ! The sale of Falteyn had not been in vain. Meshech Pelem, one of Jabavu's school friends at Healdtown, wrote in later years : " His greatness is based on the excellent character of his mother. I remember the hard struggle she had washing and carrying laundry to get money to educate her son."

At Home in King Williamstown

The young Jabavus set up house in King Williamstown. There four sons were born to them. The house was a centre of hospitality. The Sunday dinner table resounded with happy laughter. To the end of his days, Jabavu loved a joke. The household met twice daily for family worship. There was a mimosa tree in the garden where the father often went for prayer.

Mr. Jabavu bore a very high character in the town. " There are no whisperings about him," a local paper once said. He became a member of the Wesleyan Conference in 1883 and held almost every Church office in which a layman could serve. He was a circuit steward for nearly thirty years. He gave time and money without stint. He furthered the building of churches and the training of ministers. In later life he was greatly attracted to the Society of Friends.

In 1891 he began an evening school in King Williamstown. There were wonderful results. Here is one. A wild, heathen lad named Mbiko came to the night school in spite of opposition at home. He made friends, and learned to read and write. He listened to Jabavu's teaching and became a Christian and was baptised. Then he began to work. He first won his brother, then his married sisters and their husbands. At last his mother and his father became Christians too. Friends and acquaintances were reached until the whole neighbourhood was influenced. In the end Richard Mbiko became a trusted local preacher. That night school was certainly worth while.

Elda Jabavu, after more than fourteen years of happy married life, died in 1900. She had shared in her husband's interests and helped in his work. Not long after, the busy editor, beset by public and private duties, married again. His second wife and her three daughters survived him.

As the Jabavu boys grew up, their father wanted to give them every chance. He applied for the admission of the eldest to Dale College, a good public school in King Williamstown. The managers regretfully declined. They could not admit one Native boy and refuse all others. If they opened the school to both races, then the European boys would be withdrawn. The incident got into the papers. People took sides. It became clear that fuller education must be provided for Africans in their own land. Lovedale Institution was splendid but it could not do enough. It was not fair that clever Native boys should have to be sent to America or Europe for education, from lack of opportunity at home. Tengo Jabavu was one of those who took a leading part in plans to meet this need.

Before the new scheme took shape, the boy who was

excluded from Dale College was sent to school in England. He matriculated and graduated at London University in due course. He took further specialised training in England and went to North America to study Booker Washington's agricultural and industrial work among Negroes at Tuskegee Institution. He returned to his father, and to educational work in South Africa, in 1914. It was a repetition, on a larger scale and in the second generation, of what Ntwanambi and Mary Mpinde had done for their eldest son.

This is the home background of the great Bantu patriot. Before we turn to his public life let us make a picture of him in our minds. He is a big, burly man with his father's broad features and his mother's intelligent air. He speaks in a deep bass voice. His eyes are fearless and piercing. He is grave and dignified in speech and manner. Yet he is cheerful and makes the best of what comes. He does not seek great things for himself. He is said to know more people than any other Native in South Africa, and he dearly loves his friends. But he is apt to be overbearing in argument. He does not know how to speak the soft word which turns away wrath. He trusts men freely and completely. But if they deceive him he finds it hard to forgive and forget.

The Press and the College

Mr. Jabavu's largest service for his country was through his editorship of *Imvo*, and his share in founding the South African Native College at Fort Hare. His journal, *Imvo*, set itself to a double task. It had to *express* Native opinion, and it had to *instruct and inform it*. The Bantu people of South Africa often felt that their interests were in danger. White men did not always understand. Proposals were made about land which interfered with Native welfare. Laws which seemed unfair were presented to Parliament. Sometimes justice was not done in cases where Natives were concerned. When people feel like this it is dangerous if they have no means of expression. In *Imvo* the South African Bantu found their voice.

But *Imvo* had also to instruct its readers. Jabavu had made a careful study of political affairs. The Natives as a whole had little experience in such matters. Many of them did not know how to use the power they had been given, nor how to work to get more. In the pages of *Imvo* Jabavu helped them to understand the Government's methods of work. He showed how a vote should be used. He helped in the choice of right candidates for office. He fought against bribery in any form. He stood for combined action.

One deep conviction lay behind all Mr. Jabavu's work. He held that black and white were meant to help one another. He believed in the capacity of men of good will in both races. In his mind their real interests were not opposed. " He did great service not only to the race from which he sprang but to the whole community, both white and black. He was a link between them. He enabled each to understand something of the nature, feelings, and interests of the other." So wrote an English member of Parliament who was one of Jabavu's personal friends. But while *Imvo* was always used as a bridge between the two races, the Editor was splendidly courageous in his work. He did not join either black or white in needless complaint of one another. But where he saw injustice he exposed it in burning words.

Again and again he won causes for his people, in face of what seemed impossible odds. They accepted him as leader and champion of their rights. Only once, when he was getting old, did their confidence in him break. He supported a Parliamentary Bill which they strongly opposed ; he did. not know how to explain to them the situation as he saw it and never quite regained their trust. This was his one serious political mistake. He gained and held to the last the ear of the responsible white officials. They listened, even when they did not agree with his views. They trusted his character, knowing he did not serve any private ends. The Prime Minister of the Union of South Africa wrote after his death : " The name of Tengo Jabavu is a household word throughout South Africa. . . . The sanity of his outlook and integrity of his character commanded respect. His ability as a man and his skill as a journalist compelled admiration." He was recognised in the Legislative Assembly as one of the few leader writers in South Africa who could control and form public opinion. " He filled a unique place in the land," wrote one of the Commissioners for Native Affairs.

The inauguration of the South African Native College at Fort Hare owed more to Tengo Jabavu than to any other Bantu. Strong influences were moving towards the provision of higher education for the Bantu. The incident at Dale College in King Williamstown had not been forgotten. The great Principal Stewart of Lovedale was full of the idea of an inter-state Native College to meet the need of all South Africa. Before his death in 1905 he had charged Jabavu to support the scheme. The South African Native Affairs Commission (1903) recommended in its report that such a College be established.

Large representative Conventions met at Lovedale in 1905 and again three years later to make plans. Speakers, both Native and European, were sent out. Mr. Jabavu, with others, visited towns in Cape Colony, the Orange Free State, the Transvaal, and Basutoland. The National Council or *Pitso* (see p. 22) in Basutoland were so keen about the College that they promised £6,000. The Transkeian Territories General Council promised £10,000.

Jabavu worked in all directions. In *Imvo* he vigorously advocated the scheme and defended it when attacked. When he went to London in 1911 to the Universal Races Congress, he urged the need for the College. He rejoiced when in 1913 the third Convention of representatives decided to open work with such funds as were in hand. He was active in securing Fort Hare, about a mile from Lovedale Institution, as the site of the college. He ceaselessly drew in interest and enlisted the support of Churches and Missions. Perhaps his greatest joy was the appointment of his eldest son, just returned from England and America, as the first lecturer on the College staff. He was present at the inauguration of the College by General Botha in February, 1916.

Tengo Jabavu's views on educational questions were clear. Two women applied for admission to the new college when the first enrolments were being made. The buildings were not completed ; the Principal did not see how women could be fitted in. But to Jabavu's mind the policy of giving men an education from which women were excluded was wrong. For the sake of his people he took up the cause of the two women. And he carried his point. Ever since there have been women as well as men students at Fort Hare. It is admitted that Mr. Jabavu was right.

He also stood for giving ministers as good an education as was offered to professional men. He did not rest until the new college invited the various Churches to open hostels where theological students might live. Thus they had both the teaching of their own Church and the general advantages of the College education and discipline. Most well-informed South Africans would agree with what the *Christian Express* (now the *South African Outlook*) said of Tengo Jabavu's educational work.

For the advancement of his people he looked more to education than to anything else. . . . He sat as a member of the Provincial Education Commission on Native Education in 1919. He was, with three fellow-members, the first of the Native people appointed to membership of a Government Commission. But perhaps his greatest service to Native education was in connection with the South African Native College at Fort Hare. From the first day that he envisaged the scheme until the day of his death it commanded his strength. He attended Convention after Convention. . . . As a member of the Executive we believe he was never absent from a single meeting . . . no call of private business or even dangerous weakness of health ever prevented him from attending the Government Council. . . . To many of the Native people he stood, as it were, the head of the College, which they called *I-Koleji ka Jabavu* (Jabavu's College).

Mr. Jabavu's health was broken even before the College at Fort Hare had opened and begun its work. But he struggled on bravely against recurring illness for some years. In September, 1921, he travelled with difficulty to Fort Hare to attend a committee meeting. There, while staying in the house of his eldest son, he peacefully died.

No one is so fitted to sum up the values of this Bantu patriot's life as Mr. R. W. Rose-Innes of King Williamstown. From the day when he first backed the finances of *Imvo* he had been an honoured and a faithful friend. He wrote :

In the early hours of Saturday, September 10th, there passed away at Fort Hare, somewhat unexpectedly, and amid many manifestations of regret and sorrow, a notable personality. Mr. Jabavu was a man of high character, of wide influence, and of great ability. He was a keen politician. He was a man who for many years exercised both might and power among his confrères and throughout the Union of South Africa. It will be a matter of great difficulty to replace Mr. Jabavu in the editorship of *Imvo* as the wise, moderate, far-seeing counsellor of his countrymen ; on the Council of the South African Native College ; and in the offices which he faithfully filled from youth upward in the Wesleyan Church. Courteous always ; temperate in the expression of his views and sympathies which he tenaciously held to the last ; bold and courageous where boldness and courage were needed ; self-effacing and yet self-respecting ; modest and yet outspoken—his death at sixty-two years of age will be mourned by many. . . . A long and faithful discharge of duty is a fine memorial.

JAMES EMMAN KWEGYIR AGGREY

O N the Gold Coast and in Ashanti there have for centuries past been Royal Linguists attached to kings and chiefs. Their duty has been not only to interpret languages but to interpret questions that arise. When men disagreed and brought a case to be tried, the chief had a Linguist to help him to find out the truth. When strangers came to court, the Linguist interpreted them and the king to one another. When questions arose between tribe and tribe, or between Africans and white men, the Linguist could often turn the issue either to peace or to war. The office of Linguist or interpreter was one of high honour. Some Linguists made a mark in the history of their time.

There was on the Gold Coast in the nineteenth century a man named Kodwo Kwegyir Aggrey, who was Royal Linguist in the court of King Amonu V of Anamabu. He not only served his master, a Fanti chief, very faithfully, but he won honour at the court of the great Ashanti king. In time of war he could travel when roads were closed to trade. When men began to quarrel he could often make peace. The Africans and the British officials both trusted him ; he helped them to understand one another.

In the year 1875 there was born to this Linguist a son —James Emman Kwegyir Aggrey—who became one of the greatest interpreters ever known. He went out into three continents—Africa, America, and Europe—giving his life to help people to understand one another.

117

Before we tell his story, let us look at three pictures of him at his interpreter's work.

First, in America. It is the month of September, 1921. In a beautiful hotel, high up among woods and mountains where Red Indians used to dwell, some seventy men and women are gathered for a week. They have come from America, North and South; from many countries of Europe; Asia has sent Chinese, Indians, and Japanese. Two sons of Africa are there: an American Negro, Dr. R. R. Moton of Tuskegee, and Dr. J. E. Kwegyir Aggrey—our Interpreter. It is a meeting of the International Missionary Council; they are discussing how the message of the Christians' gospel may be made real to every race. See— Dr. Aggrey, slender, eager, with flashing eye, swift gesture, and ready smile, has risen and is speaking. Men laugh as they listen, and then come near to tears. He thinks the white man has failed in understanding the black man, and he proves his point. He unfolds the mind of an African so that men of other lands comprehend. He interprets the treasures of his people, their pride in being " black, black, black." He sits down, having opened a new vision of Africa; the whole Council has seen it and can never forget.

Second, in London, three years later. A number of new missionaries are being sent out by the Wesleyan Church. A great central hall is thronged with those who have come to say farewell. The address is to be given by one who was taught in boyhood by a missionary, who saw his home become Christian through missionary work—our Interpreter again. He tells how the Christian message is stirring African tribes; he interprets his people's need—" We want to know; we want to know; we want to be educated "; he pictures the love which is born for missionaries who, like their Master Christ, forget themselves. " The missionary who does the greatest job is the one who is not only a Christian but a Christ."

" He was," wrote one who was present, " the embodiment of the African spirit—eloquent, vivacious, passionate, pathetic, but he drove the reporters to despair. How can

you report a man's hands ? Dr. Aggrey literally speaks
with hands as well as voice. Of course he carried everything
before him."

Third, in Africa. An inland town in the Gold Coast
Colony : a large hastily erected building thronged to its
utmost : chiefs great and lesser in clusters at the front :
tribesmen, old, middle-aged, and young from all the country-

DR. AGGREY WITH AN ENGLISH BOY FRIEND.
Photo by Hubert W. Peet.

side crowding to hear a man—one of themselves in race
and sympathy—standing to speak. It is our Interpreter.
He has come up from the Government College at Achimota
to which he has given his life. Untrue stories have been
set on foot about that College : he has come to explain
its purpose, to interpret the mind of its principal and staff.
With what skill he builds a bridge between his people who
want to know and those who have come to teach them.

He bends his wit and eloquence to bring white and black together in co-operation for Africa's good.

The meeting is over, but see! the chiefs gather the leading men. They understand now about the College, but they want to know about the little local schools. Can they be made better? Can they work to prepare the best village boy and girl to go up to college one day? The Interpreter laughs for joy as he listens. How he hoped they would ask him that! He talks, and talks again as they question him; it is two o'clock in the morning before he and his audience have had enough.

His African Home

Of his father the Linguist we have already told. His mother—active still but aged—was living in 1928 when these stories were written, cherished by those who knew her famous son. She came of high Fanti family, Kwegyir, her eldest son, being heir to the five " stools " of her house. It was a happy home; the Aggrey family had many friends. Kwegyir was a merry boy, full of laughter, ready for endless games with other boys on the seashore. He went to a mission school. He must have worked as hard as he played, for at eight years old he could read the Bible, and as he tells us himself, used to put the Book under his pillow that he might dream of it at night. The father never tired of asking the bright boy questions, and at last he and all the family became Christians, to Kwegyir's great joy.

When the boy was about thirteen he went to live with other boys in the missionary's own house. It also was a happy home. There he learned one great lesson which he never forgot. He told the story long years after. The missionary started to cross the courtyard one sunny day without a hat. His wife saw him and called him back. He hesitated for a moment, but he knew she was right, so he yielded his will to hers and did as she asked. The keen-eyed boy who was watching saw it all. " When I have a wife of my own," he said to himself, " I will treat her like that." And he did.

In 1890 the boy had passed his standards and was chosen to start a little bush school. His mother saw that he had enough neat clothing; he took also a dozen books, two loaves of bread, a little sugar, and a small sum of money given him by friends. This was Kwegyir Aggrey's modest start in life. He and his missionary friend walked off into the bush together. The first night they slept in a little chapel, one in the pulpit, the other on a bench. The next night there was one small bed which they shared.

The little school was soon established. When it was prospering the young teacher was called back to more important work. In course of time he became the head of the principal Wesleyan school at Cape Coast Castle. He got his pupils to work as hard as he worked himself. The whole 300 of them passed the government examination with 100 per cent. marks, three months ahead of the time table. The Director of Education was pleasantly surprised.

All through life Dr. Aggrey was distinguished for his industry. With him brilliance never took the place of hard work. In his early days teaching and learning went hand in hand. He won five teacher's certificates, going on from grade to grade. He studied for the Christian ministry and finished his course when he was eighteen. He was just going to be admitted as a minister when he himself reminded the Wesleyan Synod that, according to their rules, he was four years too young.

When workshops were added to the school he threw himself into the various industries. For his own pleasure he learned, like John Tengo Jabavu (see p. 108), to be a working printer. He had a great gift for languages, both those of Africa and afterwards of Europe. The mission called for his help in translating sacred songs and hymns into the Fanti language; the British Government took him as interpreter on one of their military expeditions to Ashanti.

In 1897 Kodwo Aggrey died, full of years and of honour. His death-bed was lit by visions of the future before his son. The words which he spoke were never forgotten by that son. Within a few weeks of his own sudden death in 1927,

J. E. Kwegyir Aggrey was recalling those sacred moments and planning one day to write his father's life.

It was not long before the future which the father had foreseen opened before his son. With the advice and help of friends the young man, having said good-bye to his mother, went to the United States of America in 1898, not returning to Africa for more than twenty years.

His American Home

Young Aggrey went to Livingstone College, Salisbury, in North Carolina, one of the Southern States. It was a fine institution, standing in large grounds. It had over three hundred students coming from Africa, South America, and the West Indies, as well as from the Negroes in the United States. Here Kwegyir Aggrey at once took a leading place.

Like many African students he had more brains in his head than money in his pocket. He had to work hard to keep himself at college. His knowledge of printing came in of use. He used to say he made himself " blacker than ever " with printers' ink. He became a journalist in his vacations and wrote for several newspapers. He took his B.A. degree brilliantly in 1902.

In Salisbury, as on the Gold Coast, while he studied he taught. Generation after generation of students passed through his hands in the twenty years he was at Livingstone College. The boys loved him, as he loved them. He was their friend. He encouraged them in self-support and in all worthy ambition. He was quite sorry for a boy if his father paid all his fees at school.

It is almost bewildering to follow all that this eager, merry, hardworking man set himself to do. He took his M.A. and his D.D. degree in Salisbury. In one summer vacation after another he attended the Summer Session at the University of Columbia in New York, always doing well. It cost him strenuous work and real self-denial to provide the fees. He helped in the preparation of Negro teachers for government examinations. Having studied

for the ministry he gladly undertook pastoral work in
rural districts among very poor Negro people. Years
afterwards, when on tour in Africa, he told a group of
African students at Lovedale Institution something of how
he did this work in the Southern States.

I went to the country to preach. I could quote Hebrew,
Greek, and Latin, but what did my people care about that?
I was in the aeroplane and I had to come down. I started preaching on " Give ye them to eat "—preaching chicken, sheep, something to eat, something to wear. I had a sermon on angels. I
told them that mosquitoes, flies, and so on, were messengers sent
from God. Mosquitoes come to say " There is death round here,
I am talking to you; don't you hear me? As long as you don't
hear me, the swamp stays and will give you disease. Clean it."
Then the mosquitoes sing another song: " Let thy servant
depart in peace."
We had a look-out committee. They found an old lady who
had no wood for her fire. They said " She won't come to church."
I sent workers to get wood for people like that and then they
began to come to church. If you practise the kind of Christianity
that goes round helping people they will say Amen.
At one chapel the people were very poor. . . . I told my
people I was going to come and stay in their homes. They slept
eight or ten in a room with the windows stopped up, they were
afraid of the night air. I asked if I could open one a little bit.
I said " Next year I am going to take a census of the chickens
that you raise; the meat is good and the eggs are the best food
for man or child."

Dr. Aggrey did this work because he loved it; his
warm human sympathies brought him close to those in
need. He did not yet see that it was preparing him to meet
a great new call.
America had given the brilliant young African much.
But the best remains to be told. There in Salisbury was
set up another Aggrey home, sweet and peaceful as that on
the Gold Coast, where in cultured simplicity a young father
and mother gathered children round them giving them the
priceless heritage of a happy home. In 1905 J. E. Kwegyir
Aggrey married Rose Rudolph Douglass, of African race

but long domiciled in Virginia. Like him she was a distinguished graduate and a teacher in Livingstone College. She shared every interest of his life.

ALL ROUND AFRICA

Had he forgotten Africa, this man round whom home, wife, children, and work had drawn so closely in the New World ? Not so. Africa was always in his heart. At last the time came when all he had learned in his busy life was claimed for his own land.

All Africa was asking for education. Everywhere governments and missions were trying to respond. A call came from the simple African people who wanted to make their homes better and to get more produce from their land. They wanted to understand the changes which were round them, that they and their children might play a part in their country's life. The little bush schools where an untrained teacher tried to instruct them did not help them much.

Another call came from African boys who were passing quickly through the school standards, and wanted to learn some trade or calling, or perhaps, if they had ability, to be teachers or professional men. They were growing restless and dissatisfied for lack of outlet ; they had powers they did not know how to use.

A call came from the African girls and women, and from their fathers and husbands and brothers, who wished them to be taught. They wanted to learn home-making and the care of children, how to nurse the sick or teach a school, and some of them could learn to train other women to serve the home and the community. Perhaps the call of the girls and women was loudest of all.

A group of men in North America and Great Britain, who loved Africa and believed in the power of education, resolved to respond to the call. They offered, first, to send a Commission [1] to see what was needed in Africa, and what was being done. Everybody there was ready to welcome

[1] Known as the Phelps-Stokes Education Commission to Africa.

them—government officials and missionaries and the Africans too. Two parties went out: the first in 1920 went to West and South Africa, the second in 1924 to Abyssinia, East and Central Africa, and to South Africa again.

Two men were members of both Commissions. One was the Chairman, Dr. Thomas Jesse Jones, an American. The other was our African Interpreter, Dr. Aggrey himself. Dr. Jones had long known him and his work. There was no other African with such fitness for the great and delicate task. In country after country the Commissions gave help to schools and all those who were responding to Africa's call. The reports of the two Educational Commissions fill two large volumes. But here we can only speak of Dr. Aggrey's share.

He was an interpreter indeed. It was like travelling with Africa to have him in the group, with his happy laughter, his gaiety, his child-like spirit, his fearless and confident trust. He made light of difficulties and never shirked hard work. When he was slighted or rebuffed by strangers because he was an African, he took it patiently and turned the cross into a crown.

" God knew what He was doing when He made me black," he often said. " He didn't want me to be grey or white but just black. On the piano you can't play a good tune with the white notes alone ; you must have the black ones too. God wants to play tunes with His white and His black notes together."

Every member of each Commission learned to know him as a real friend.

But if he helped white men to understand the African he gave himself with equal eagerness to make the African understand the white man. They were both his friends and he introduced them to one another. In some places he found strain between his own people and the authorities. Because of his loyalty to both he was able to go to and fro putting a healing hand on sore places and letting in wholesome light and air. In one colony after another he gained the confidence of officials, settlers, and missionaries, winning a place given to no other Son of Africa. He never used this privilege for any end of his own, but only for his fellow Africans.

His welcome on the Gold Coast was a great event. People who had known him as a boy flocked to do him honour. He was dressed by them in resplendent robes. He was escorted to the market-place at Anamabu, bands playing, flags flying, great state umbrellas swaying in the sun. He was installed as Royal Linguist in succession to his father. Speeches of welcome were made. But to Kwegyir Aggrey the supreme joy of his visit to the Gold Coast was meeting with his mother, after two and twenty years.

Some who read these stories may remember the day when the Commission visited their school. Some may have heard Dr. Aggrey speak. Certainly the boys in Uganda will not have forgotten the story of the Eagle and the Chickens which he told them one day. They will like to share it with all young Africans here.

The Story of the Eagle and the Chickens

A certain man went through a forest and caught a young eagle. He brought it home, put it among his fowls and ducks and turkeys, and gave it chickens' food to eat. Yet all the while it was an eagle, the king of birds.

Some time later a naturalist came to see him. Passing through the garden he said, " That bird is an eagle, not a chicken."

" Yes," said the owner, " but I have trained it to be a chicken. It is no longer an eagle ; it has become a chicken, even though it measures fifteen feet from tip to tip of its wings."

" No," said the naturalist, " it is an eagle still. It has the heart of an eagle, and I will make it soar high up to the heavens."

But the owner persisted, " The eagle has become a chicken ; it will never fly."

They agreed to test which was right. The naturalist picked up the eagle, held it high and said : " Eagle, thou art an *eagle ;* thou dost belong to the sky and not to this earth. Stretch forth thy wings and fly."

The eagle turned this way and that. But down below it were the chickens picking up their food. In a moment it was by their side.

The owner said, " I told you it was a chicken."

" No," said the naturalist, " it is an eagle. Give it to-morrow another chance."

So the next day the bird was taken to the top of the house, a little further from where the chickens were. " Eagle, thou art an eagle ; stretch forth thy wings and fly." But again the chickens were in sight and they were feeding. The eagle alighted and fed with them.

" I told you it was a chicken," said the owner again. But still the man who knew asserted, " No ; it is an eagle and has still an eagle's heart. To-morrow I will make it fly."

Next morning he rose early and took the eagle outside the city, away from the houses, to the foot of a high mountain. The sun was just rising, gilding the top of the mountain and making each crag glisten in the glory of the new day. " Eagle, thou art an eagle ; thou dost belong to the sky and not to this earth. Stretch forth thy wings and fly." Held high, the eagle looked around and trembled, but still it did not fly.

Then the man, who knew the ways of birds, turned it till it faced the sun. Suddenly it stretched out its wings and with the wild scream of a free and sun-loving eagle it mounted up higher and higher and never returned.

It was an eagle all the time, though it had eaten chickens' food.

" My people of Africa," said Dr. Aggrey, when he had told his story, " we were created in the image of God, but men have made us think that we are chickens and not capable of improvement. We still think this is true. *But we are eagles.* Stretch forth your wings and fly. Some of you will say, ' I must have three or four wives.' Man, you are not a chicken but an eagle ; your home is in heaven. Stretch forth your wings by the power of God and fly. Don't be content with chickens' food."

To the Gold Coast Again

The Interpreter, when he came back from his second African journey, was ready for new work. Where could best use be made of his experience and of his gifts ? That was what his friends in America, in Great Britain, and in Africa asked. He was a man of three continents now.

America offered him the principalship of an important college. South Africa would have welcomed him and his family at the great Training Institution at Lovedale, and

Aggrey had given much of his heart to South Africa. But the call which came from the British Government and the Gold Coast seemed to be the end to which all his previous life converged.

At Achimota, about eight miles inland from Accra, not far from where he was born, a great site had been set apart on a grassy hillside for a college for Africans. It seemed to bring all his highest dreams, and the dreams of the two Commissions, towards fulfilment. And the man whom the British Government chose to give shape to the plan— Principal A. G. Fraser—knew Dr. Aggrey and loved him. He said he would not go to Achimota without Dr. Aggrey at his side.

Those were busy days in London, consulting over plans. In and out of the Colonial Office in Downing Street went the fair-haired Scotsman and the dark African, in perfect team work, pulling the same way. There grew up between them a comradeship of loyalty and affection which never failed. In September, 1924, they sailed with others for Achimota.

The Achimota site was large. The buildings were to be numerous. The staff was to be unusually large and highly qualified. There was money to do things which were impossible in most mission schools. The scheme was attracting notice everywhere. But none of these things drew Dr. Aggrey to Achimota. Here is what he said himself.

The Achimota tradition, if one may use that word of this new college, is that of service for country ; of co-operation irrespective of colour ; of education of head, hand, and heart. Our aim is to take all the best in African culture and combine it with the best in the culture of the West.

African history, art, music, folk-lore, and Native customs and laws were to be studied and taught. The staff began to work on them at once while studying the languages of the people.

The students were to begin as tiny children, boys and girls together. Side by side with class-room studies

agriculture was to be part of normal life. All were to share
in the joy of the workshop and the dignity of home industry.
Service for their country, and for the world, was to be the
goal of advance in knowledge. Achimota aimed at helping
Africa to get the best out of everything and especially out
of herself. The whole plan rested on a belief in the supreme
importance of Christian character and its expression in
life and in the worship of God. This had always been Dr.
Aggrey's gospel. It was a gospel which many a school in
Africa was striving to preach. But here at Achimota, on
a large scale and in the eyes of the world, there was a chance
of making a great new beginning.

Clear and fair the ideal shone before the whole staff at
Achimota, even through the discomfort and confusion of
early days. Roads were being made, water brought in
pipes, houses and class-rooms built, playing fields laid out.
For the first year accommodation was scanty ; all the staff
had to live in one house. Principal Fraser and Dr. Aggrey
shared a room. Later a house was found in Accra where
Mrs. Aggrey joined her husband, until lack of health compelled her return to America. At last Dr. Aggrey's own
house in the College grounds was ready, and he settled in
to work. Here is a picture of him from a European colleague
who lived next door.

His house was next to mine. I know the life he lived. Up
early, reading and writing through half the night, eating at the
longest intervals and eating almost nothing then, always working,
never resting, constantly interrupted. He filled his crowded
days with labour. And four times a month he would be away on
long journeys to distant places where two or three days would
be spent in exhausting speeches and still more exhausting talk.

It was on one of these visits that we first saw our
Interpreter at work (see p. 119). When Fourah Bay College
in Sierra Leone had its centenary in 1926, Aggrey was sent
up with greetings from Achimota. Here, where Samuel
Adjai Crowther had been the first student one hundred years
before (see p. 68), the Interpreter from the Gold Coast
drew thousands to hear his wise and burning words.

A splendid life of service was opening before Kwegyir Aggrey at Achimota. Principal Fraser's conviction that his influence would secure close co-operation with the chiefs and other leading Africans had proved true. The Governor of the Gold Coast—Sir Gordon Guggisberg, since retired—gave his friendship and confidence to Dr. Aggrey. When the Prince of Wales came to open the College he had a long talk with this African who was at the heart of the work.

In 1927, Dr. Aggrey was given six months' leave of absence. He wanted—with intense longing—to see his wife and family in North Carolina, especially the little baby son born since Mrs. Aggrey left Africa. And he wanted to finish a thesis which had to be written before he could claim his degree as Doctor of Philosophy from Columbia University. The necessary examinations he had already passed. Into that book he wanted to gather the fruit of what he had learned in America, what he had seen in Africa, and what he had to say to the white people and the black people about one another. He meant to tell the story of what his friend the Governor had done for the Gold Coast.

On his way to America he spent a few weeks in England, rejoicing in the fellowship of many friends. He talked of his home, and of his book. And he talked much of these *Lives of Eminent Africans*, and read some of them, and helped to choose the Africans who should be given place. He wanted to use the stories in his teachers' class at Achimota; he was going to send the book to all his friends. Instead, he has come himself into its pages as one of the greatest sons Africa has given to the world.

He crossed his last ocean to the United States, spent one brief fortnight with wife and children and baby boy at Salisbury, and returned to New York to work upon his volume. There sudden illness seized him, and on the last day of July, 1927, he died, aged fifty-one years.

There was mourning in New York and in Salisbury; in London and in many places in England where Dr. Aggrey was loved. The news was cabled to Africa: at Achimota the new Governor—Sir Ransford Slater—summoned a great memorial service and took part in it himself; similar services were held at Kumasi and on the Gold Coast. The Press in Great Britain and West and South Africa bore tribute to the inter-racial service and noble character of Dr. Aggrey. Thousands sorrowed in reverent sympathy with the wife and children at Salisbury in North Carolina and with the aged mother on the Gold Coast.

A few months later Sir Gordon Guggisberg, travelling in America, went to see Dr. Aggrey's wife at Salisbury, and spoke to his old pupils in Livingstone College.

Let us take our last look at this great African through the eyes of the British Governor in whose Colony he served.

The essence of Aggrey was that he was an African, imbued with the ancient customs and traditions of his people. His knowledge of the way in which they thought was undisturbed by his Western education and his brilliant scholastic career in the United States. But his deep affection for his people and their customs never blinded him to the fact that changes must come, conditions and manner of life must alter, if his beloved Africans were to keep pace with modern civilisation in a continually advancing world. . . . His constant anxiety was how to give Africans opportunities for acquiring all the learning, all the knowledge of arts and crafts, all the mental poise and character that centuries of slow progress have given to the civilised nations of the world, and yet how to ensure that they retain the spirit of their ancestors. . . . He was the finest interpreter which the present century has produced of the white man to the black, of the black man to the white. To neither in his private conversation was he sparing in his criticism of their failings, but it was kindly criticism. . . .

I have written of my friend Aggrey as I found the man—found him in many long and very personal talks with him, found him in his work. Of all the men I know Aggrey was most prepared to cross the great river. He would not grieve except for leaving his wife and children—and his unfinished task.

There are others to come. May his example stimulate them. May we have more Aggreys in our great continent of Africa.

SHORTER STORIES

A MAN'S true greatness does not depend on the largeness of his sphere of work. It is measured by his character and his service of his fellow men. There are not many African chiefs who, like Moshoeshoe, build a nation, or like Khama, reform a tribe. There are not many prime ministers, or travellers and educators, or editors, or bishops, like Kagwa, and Aggrey and Jabavu and Crowther. But there are numbers of district chiefs, farmers, teachers, doctors, lawyers, men of commerce, artisans, office and hospital assistants who have shown in the past and show to-day in their quiet service the qualities which made the eminent Africans great.

It is such men, and the women who are in partnership with them in home and in the affairs of life, who hold the future of Africa in their hands. Here are the stories of four men who are not what history calls famous—but they certainly have been, or are, in the true sense, great.

I. CHIEF ONOYOM IYA NYA

WHY THE CANOE WAS STOPPED IN THE CREEK

The canoe of the Scottish missionary was being paddled down the Enyong Creek in Southern Nigeria. She had finished her wonderful work in Okoyong and had just been up to Arochuku, the great slave-trading centre between the Cross and the Niger rivers. It was not a likely place for a mission station. But difficulties always attracted Mary Slessor, her heart was set on planting teachers in Aro and the district round.

The creek was very lovely as the canoe glided along. Overhanging trees were reflected in the smooth water. Bright birds and butterflies flitted to and fro. As the missionary watched the busy water snakes crossing the stream something brushed against the back of her canoe. She looked round quickly. It was another smaller canoe. A man stood in it. " Ma," he said, " I have been waiting for you. My master at Akani Obio sent me to waylay you and bring you to his house." He took a letter from his cap and handed it to her.

The missionary followed up a side creek full of lilies, even lovelier than the one she had left. On a small trading beach stood a well-dressed, pleasant-faced young man and his wife. They helped her out of the canoe and led her into their house. It was a good house with concrete floors. The room was prettily furnished. Everything spoke of good taste. A cup of tea was brought. The owner of the house was Chief Onoyom Iya Nya.

The Chief told his visitor how he had watched for her on the creek. Twice he had missed her. Then he posted a man to wait till she came, and bring her to his house. Onoyom was certainly in earnest. He told his story while his wife stood by: " Ma," he said, " will you show me what to do ? " It was late that day before the missionary left the home on Akani Obio beach. Her canoe ran into a rainstorm as they paddled down the river and every one got wet. But her heart was full of warmth and gladness because of what she heard from Onoyom. Presently we shall hear how she answered his question. But first we must trace his early days.

Onoyom was born between 1860 and 1865. The Enyong district when he was a boy had little to do with the outer world. Akani Obio was on the trade route from Arochuku to Itu. All the canoes with slaves for sale had to stop at the beach to pay toll before they passed on. The canoes came regularly every fourth day. As soon as Onoyom earned a little money he went to the beach and bought his first slave.

There was of course no school for the boy. He shared

the common life of the country-side. He went with his master to work on the farm, and to buy and sell in the neighbouring markets. He learned how to grow crops and to trade. He fished and bathed in the river. He heard the talk of the old men and women and knew the folk-lore and history of his town. He went to the plays and dances and sacrificed to the juju of his tribe. He took part in tribal wars. He was just like other boys and youths in Akani Obio, except that he never touched gin and seldom even drank palm wine.

One day he was bathing at the beach when he was ten or twelve years old. A canoe came up with two white men who wanted to see the chief. The village people were frightened and ran away, but Onoyom consented to act as a guide. He listened to their palaver with the chief. The men said they were missionaries and had come from their station down the river to visit the chief. They began to tell of the message they brought. The chief was angry and ordered them to leave the town. Onoyom was brought before the headmen and punished for having shown the way.

Some years later, when Onoyom was grown up and knew many white men well, he was brought near these same missionaries again. A chief who was a friend of his was very ill. Onoyom and others took him down the river in a steam launch one Sunday morning to get fresh air. The tide was ebbing, the launch struck a sandbank and stuck fast. No release was possible for hours until the flood tide came. The sandbank was exactly opposite the little mission church. As they sat round the dying chief on deck they heard the congregation singing and could understand what the minister said as he preached.

Onoyom became a great trader and a successful farmer. He had a large household and many wives. His influence spread in the district. A chief from Calabar, who was President of the Native Court at Itu, got him made a member of the Court. He thus came to the notice of the British officials who were trying to open up the country and stop the slave-trade from Arochuku. At first when they asked him questions he was not willing to reply. Like others, he was afraid of losing the profits of the slave-trade. But when he saw that Government were working for the welfare of his people he gave all the help he could.

Up at Arochuku there was the terrible Long Juju, round which a great system of human sacrifices had been built up. Onoyom had been there himself to cannibal feasts. When Natives came in hundreds from long distances to consult the Juju, they were either sacrificed or sold as slaves. The Government decided to send up a military expedition to put an end to the cruelties. Onoyom was sent for and informed that he was to be the guide. He did his duty faithfully. The secret places of the Long Juju were opened to the light of day. After much palaver, treaties were made with the chiefs. Onoyom saw that a new day was coming. The customs of his fathers were passing away.

Though the young Chief prospered, he had trouble at home. His house was burnt down. Then his only child died. He sought the man who had, as he thought, worked this evil by witchcraft, that he might slay him. Then he met a former mission teacher from Calabar, a man who had fallen into evil ways and been dismissed. But he remembered enough to talk to Onoyom about the true God:

" Where can I find this God ? " asked the Chief.

" I am not worthy to tell you," was the reply, " but go to the white Ma at Itu and she will tell you."

" I will go," said Onoyom ; and that was why Mary Slessor's canoe was stopped in Enyong Creek.

The Town of the Rising Sun

Chief Onoyom was never " eminent " in the same sense that Moshoeshoe and Khama were. But though his sphere was in one town and district, he was certainly eminent there. In his own neighbourhood he was recognised as a ruler who was enlightened and wise. When Mary Slessor visited him he had already been chosen as President of the Native Court.

Gradually and quietly, as he listened to the answer to his question (see p. 133), he put all his influence on the

Christian side. He delighted to share the comfort and
refinement of his home with missionaries who passed up
or down the Creek. He began daily prayers in his house
and village. He determined, though he knew little of the
religion which the white men were teaching, to build a
church where he and his people could worship God. He
had saved £300 ; that should go towards the expense.
The house for God should be at least as good as one he would
build for himself. So the church had iron walls, a cement
floor, and a bell-tower. He even cut down a great juju
tree in his grounds to make the seats and pulpit. This
frightened the people. Some of them fled from the town
believing that death and destruction would surely follow.

Little by little the building grew. At last it was complete. The opening service was held on November 5th,
1905. The Chief provided food for the whole assembly.
Nothing stronger than palm wine was drunk. In order
that even in wet weather people might come to church,
Onoyom built a bridge over a swampy part of the road.
Meantime Onoyom had been learning the deeper meaning
of the Christian faith. A few days later he, his wife and
baby, and nearly forty others were baptised. The party
included one of the boys who had paddled Mary Slessor
up the Creek two and a half years before. The people
flocked to the services in the church. A white flag was
flown on Sundays to show that trading was not allowed.

It was the Chief's custom on Saturday afternoon to sit on
the verandah of his house and keep an eye on the road leading out of the village. When he saw a company evidently
leaving the town for the week-end, he called them up.
If their business did not require haste he ordered them back
to the village till Sunday was over.

A few months later a calamity did befall the town. But
it proved to be a blessing in disguise. The dry season had
passed ; the crops were all planted ; the rains began. The
river rose as usual, but soon last year's high-water mark
was passed. The waters crossed the roadway and flooded
the houses. The church could only be entered in a canoe.
The benches were under water. Of course people talked

about the juju tree that had been cut down. But the Chief was to be seen going to and fro in his canoe, examining the submerged village and noting the boundaries of the flood.

When the waters abated, he had decided that the village should be moved to higher ground. It was a gigantic task. The bush had to be cleared ; ground had to be levelled. As the new village began to take shape the people saw the wisdom of their Chief. Akani Obio had been built in an unhealthy swamp. The houses were huddled together. The place was overgrown and impossible to keep clean. The new site was in an airy place far above the floods. It was given a new name—Obio Usieri, the Town of the Rising Sun.

The Chief made the plans himself. The church, the school, and his own house were in the middle of the main street. Opposite to them were a playground for children and a football field for the boys. The side streets were regular and about ten yards wide. A lamp hung outside each house and was lit in the evening. " Here," said the Chief, " we have new surroundings and new dwellings ; we can begin our life anew."

Onoyom cared for the welfare of his people. He raised the whole level of their life. He opened roads that they might get easily to the farms and bring their goods to market. He cleared the waterways so that trade was increased. This brought health and contentment, and a hopeful outlook on life. The Chief wanted every child in his little town to be educated. So the school was his constant care. He spent time and money on it himself. He was most courteous in his ways. A missionary notes that he always rose and gave his seat to his wife if she came into the room where he was sitting.

As President of the Native Court Onoyom won the confidence of the people. They did not want their cases tried on a day when he was away. He was always just. He did right between man and man. He was called " a man of truth." One day there was a dispute between a slave and his master. The master was powerful and he

was Onoyom's friend, but justice was on the side of the
slave. Onoyom gave the verdict in his favour and told
the master plainly where he had been wrong.

The busy Chief was an active worker for his Church.
Men facing the cost of becoming Christians went to him for
advice. The humblest inquirer was welcomed and given
food if the Chief could not see him at once. Onoyom
often preached in his own village and in others round. He
opened many centres where Christian teaching was given.
He lent his canoe and his boys to take the missionaries to
Arochuku, and himself went to help in starting a mission
there. The words he spoke and the life he lived matched
each other.

The Chief died in February, 1924. One Saturday he
sold his cocoa in Itu market and seemed quite well. On
Sunday he told the elders of the Church of a dream in which
he had seen a big tree with others standing round it.
Suddenly the big tree fell to the ground, pulled up by the
roots. The smaller trees were unharmed. He interpreted
the dream to mean that something serious would happen
in Obio Usiere. In a few hours he was taken ill. No
treatment relieved him. On Tuesday he wrote a letter of
good-bye to his missionary friends. On Wednesday he
set his house in order, bade the elders take care of the
children, the old people, the teachers, and the strangers in
the town. In his last words he committed the church to
their care.

Thus Chief Onoyom Iya Nya died, having finished his
course.

II. J. CLAUDIUS MAY

Year after year many schools have their Speech Day.
Sometimes one of these is marked by a special event. This
was the case at Freetown, Sierra Leone, when the Wesleyan
Boys' High School met in April, 1927, after fifty-three years'
work. On that day, in the presence of a large company, a
mural tablet in memory of the first Principal was unveiled
by the Governor of the Colony. His portrait had already

been presented during his lifetime at the semi-jubilee in
1899. The Director of Education was in the Chair. He
spoke of the new plans for education in the Colony. Sierra
Leone is to share in all that modern education offers Africa.
But most of the speaking was about the past. The
Rev. J. Claudius May, the first Principal, died twenty-five
years ago, but his memory is still green and fresh. And
behind him stands his father, Joseph May, one of the early
worthies of Sierra Leone. Not only Sierra Leone but all
West Africa from Gambia to the Congo is sprinkled with
pupils of the two Mays, or their daughters and sons.

Joseph May was born about 1817 in the Yoruba country.
His father was a priest of the god Ifa. The boy was captured
in a tribal war and sold to a Portuguese slaver. The slave
ship was seized by a British man-of-war, the boy was taken
to Freetown in Sierra Leone, where Samuel Adjai Crowther
had been landed five years before. He was sent to school
and learned quickly. Afterwards he went to Fourah Bay
College, where he met Crowther (see p. 68). Later on
he worked with him as school assistant. He was sent to
England for fuller education at the Borough Road College
in London. In 1842 he returned to educational work in
Sierra Leone.

Many of his pupils made their mark in the history of
the Colony. Among them was Samuel (afterwards Sir
Samuel) Lewis, the distinguished lawyer and public servant,
a man of high character and great ability. Joseph May was
minister in the Wesleyan Church and held several important
charges. He was the first African to be chaplain to the
forces. His energy was unflagging. He spent his spare
time in learning fresh tribal languages in which to preach.
He died highly honoured and respected in 1891.

J. Claudius May, born in 1846, moved from place to
place with his parents as a child. At school he was shrewd
and intelligent, a pleasant boy to teach. At the age of
fourteen he was put into a large business house owned by
one of his father's friends. He soon mastered the whole
business. His success was due to the care he gave to details,
and to his thoroughness and sense of honour. He was made

principal accountant and largely managed the whole concern. In this business house his powers of organisation and
administration were developed. The training served him
well in after-life, though he did not become a merchant in
the end.

Friends were watching the boy as he grew up. They
wanted him to go to England for education. But his wise
mother did not wish him to go too early so far from home.
The year 1865, however, found him on his way to England,
to the college in London where his father had been twenty-
five years before. He was then nineteen. Claudius had
saved the greater part of the money needed to pay his
expenses in England. Afterwards he went to Queen's
College, Taunton.

J. Claudius May was a schoolmaster by descent and by
natural gift. He now became one by choice. The Wesleyan
Church in Sierra Leone wanted to establish a High School
for boys. In J. Claudius May they saw the first Principal.
An offer was made to him by letter. He responded to the
call. He entered Westminster College, took some Normal
training, and matriculated at London University. All
through this period Samuel Lewis, his father's former pupil,
was his intimate friend.

One April morning in 1874 the High School opened at
7 a.m. with eight boys on the roll. When the mural tablet
was unveiled in memory of the first Principal the school had
grown to a great company. Other duties gathered closely
round May as years went by. He was, like his father, a
minister. He became a member of the Board of Education,
and was offered the post of H.M. Inspector of Schools, but
declined it. He was examiner of candidates for the Civil
Service of the Colony. He was editor of a paper too. But
his crowning labour was the Boys' High School. To it he
gave his best with unswerving devotion for five and twenty
years. He married twice, and died in 1902, aged fifty-six.
Four of his children survived him. .

How did this schoolmaster so live and work as to keep
his memory alive for a quarter of a century ? What young
teacher does not want to catch his secret and be kept in

remembrance too ? To Principal May teaching was not a trade but a vocation. He taught for his boys and for Africa, not for himself. Success in life was not what he sought first for his boys. He wanted their real good, not merely their gain in money or in fame. Formation, rather than information, was the purpose of education—so he often said. He was not satisfied about a boy until he saw habits of industry, self-denial, and thrift begin to appear.

The Principal could always get alongside dull boys and help them to understand. Those who really tried were encouraged, even if they did not succeed. If ever he failed to keep discipline he looked for the weakness in himself rather than in the class. He never punished in anger. He aimed at restoring the moral strength of a boy who had done wrong. He believed in boys and looked for the best in all.

He was also a man of the sort boys love. He was on a big scale, in body, mind, and heart. He was quite fair ; they could trust him never to be unjust. He cared about their sports and encouraged manly exercise. He lived as an all-round, well-balanced Christian. The boys saw in his life a pattern they wanted to copy in their own. These are some of the reasons why J. Claudius May won intense and lasting loyalty from his boys.

III. THE STORY OF WILLIAM KOYI

Boys and girls in South Africa know about the cattle-killing delusion which broke the power of the great Xosa people in 1857. They remember how a strange message was supposed to come from the spirits of the Xosa ancestors. The people were told to slaughter all their cattle and destroy all their grain. If they did this, it was said that on a certain day the sun would rise blood-red and stand still when it reached the zenith. Then abundance of fat cattle and choice corn would suddenly spring out of the earth. Old people would get young again. The ancestral chiefs would return and rule. This was the prophecy.

Some of the Xosa believed it at once. Then the others

believed with them. Only a few had doubts. Thousands
of cattle were slaughtered each day. The growing crops
were destroyed. Store places were prepared for the splendid
cattle and the quantities of corn that were to come. The
day fixed in the prophecy arrived. The sun rose—and set.
By evening it was plain to the simple people that the
prophecy was a great deception and had brought them to
ruin. Thousands died of starvation. The British went to
help the Xosa and saved numbers of lives. This great
calamity broke up many Xosa homes. The people had
no food and were driven out into the world to look for work.

One Xosa lad named Koyi, who lived in a heathen home
on the Thomas river, went out at this time among the
Dutch farmers to seek his living. He was first a bullock
driver at half a crown a week. Then he worked for five
years in a place where they washed wool at Uitenhage and
rose to be overseer. After that he spent another five years
in a store at Port Elizabeth. He had never been to school,
but had taught himself to read. In 1869 he became a
Christian and joined the Wesleyan Church.

During his dinner hour at Port Elizabeth he picked up a
piece of paper one day. It was a page from the *Isigidimi
Sama Xosa*, the little Lovedale paper which Tengo Jabavu
afterwards edited (see p. 108). It told about the education
which Lovedale Institution gave. The place was one hundred
and fifty miles away. But Koyi was in earnest, so he started
on his long walk. He was admitted to Lovedale and passed
through the classes of the first, second, and third year. No
one ever had to ask Koyi to stick to his task. He always did
his best. He was chosen to be an assistant overseer of some
of the Native boarders' work.

In 1876 a challenge came to the students from Dr.
Stewart, the great Principal who had made Lovedale a power
in South Africa. He was going to a new Scottish mission
among the wild Angoni in Nyasaland. He wanted some of
the senior Lovedale students to come and help. Fourteen
offered ; of the four who were chosen William Koyi was one.
He said he was only fit to hew wood and draw water, but he
wanted to do what he could for his Master Jesus Christ.

William Koyi made his mark in Angoniland. One after another the missionaries bore tribute to his work. " He took possession of Angoniland for Christ," said one. " He is doing a noble work which no European could accomplish," said another. Knowing their language he got into close touch with the Angoni. They came to love and trust him. They called him " Chief." He often turned their anger aside from the white men. His own life was at times in peril but he knew no fear. He shared in the hopes of the missionaries. He entered into their large plans for the work.

Koyi only lived to give ten years of missionary service. As he lay dying a number of Angoni were seen coming up to the mission station with a message from the Chief. Koyi waited with longing to hear the news they brought. Was it to say that the door for the work of the mission was closed ? No ; the news was of the best. The Chief had given the work full liberty ; he agreed to the opening of schools. Koyi's face lit up as he said, " Lord, now lettest Thou Thy servant depart in peace, for mine eyes have seen Thy salvation."

Here is a story which shows the kind of man William Koyi was. The mission had not been long at Bandawe. Relations with the Angoni were quite uncertain still. News came in one day that a large war-party was on its way to attack the people round the mission station and to raid the station itself. What could be done ? Koyi offered to go out to meet the warriors. Perhaps he could turn them back. After walking several miles he found the Angoni. They had encamped near a little stream for a rest before they attacked.

In a moment, before he could speak to them, the young warriors sprang towards him and started their war-dance. It was an alarming sight, enough to frighten the brave. One word, one movement on his part might lead first to his own death and then to an attack on the mission. He watched the men dancing first in groups, then one by one. Their bodies were almost hidden by great shields. They brandished their stabbing assegais. They looked more like demons than men.

Koyi stood quite still. He was praying for wisdom, for he did not know what to do. Then he sat down, took off his boot and washed his foot in the stream. Quite leisurely he put his boot on again. The threatening dancing went on. Slowly he took off his second boot, and washed the other foot. His cool self-control amazed the warriors. They sat down. Then Koyi cheerfully remarked, " You are sensible people to rest yourselves on this hot day." The warriors burst out laughing. The danger was past.

Not only was war averted but friendship was begun. Koyi conducted some of the war party to the mission station. Then they took him off to call upon their Chief.

IV. THE STORY OF AUGUSTINE AMBALI

On the eastern coast of Lake Nyasa the village of Ngoo Bay lies on the edge of the sandy plain, between the water and the hills. There is not much to see in the village, but the eye is caught by a mud and reed building which is clearly a Christian Church. Near it stands a school, and facing both a small square mud house. The door opens, and an African priest, in his simple white cassock, comes out. He looks across to the lovely lake where the mission steamer has just come to anchor. Now his wife has joined him, and they talk together as they stand. His face is wise and kind, full of energy and peace. He is an old man, and white haired, but he shows no weakening in his powers. It is Canon Augustine Ambali, Priest in Charge of Ngoo Bay, and Mabel his wife. The steamer has come to take him to Likoma to preach the ordination sermon in the cathedral there. He is talking with Mabel of some things he wants done while he is away. That is a 1927 picture. The story of Augustine Ambali begins in 1872.

From Zanzibar to Nyasaland

In the year 1872, Ambali, then about fifteen, was in one of his father's fields in a village near the coast of Zanzibar.

Suddenly he was seized and sent far northward to Pangani, a seaport town, to be sold as a slave. Happily some relative recognised him. He was rescued and sent to his uncle, who was a small chief near Sadani. Ambali lived in one or another of his villages. His uncle was a Moslem and took the boy to pray in the mosque.

Sadani, some fifteen miles away, was the market town. There they went to buy cloth, or soap, or salt. There they took any produce they had for sale. One day a friend of his uncle's invited Ambali to walk with him to Sadani to sell some india-rubber. Suspecting nothing, and liking the prospect of a good long walk, he went. But the treacherous man had already sold him secretly. He was seized as a slave and taken to Pangani again.

This time he was not recognised and rescued. He was first hidden in a room and then put on board an Arab dhow (boat). The dhow set sail for Pemba Island, a great centre for the export of slaves. But an English gunboat was watching ; the dhow was captured and the slaves released. Ambali was taken to the British Consul at Zanzibar, Sir John Kirk, an old friend of Livingstone's. He offered to send Ambali to the Universities' Mission to be educated. Poor Ambali did not want to be captured again, so he accepted the offer. In a few days he was happily settled among boys of his own age in the Kiungani school on the island of Zanzibar. He was carefully taught, and in time became a true Christian. On his baptism he added the Christian name of Augustine to his own African name.

In 1883 a call came to the students at Kiungani like that which came to William Koyi at Lovedale seven years before (see p. 142). A new mission was to be begun in Nyasaland, on the eastern side of the lake. Who would volunteer from Kiungani ? It meant going to strange people who spoke an unknown language. But Augustine and five of his fellow students offered to go. So they started on the long journey round the coast to Quilimane and then up the Quaque, Zambezi, and Shire rivers to the lake. There was no railway from the coast to Blantyre, and no good motor roads beyond it, as there are to-day.

The pioneers were taking with them the iron plates and all the separate parts of a little steamer to be built for use on the lake. A steamer, even when it is taken to pieces, is not convenient to carry about. A large number of porters had to be brought from Zanzibar to act as carriers. Every one had to take a share of the heavy work. The leader of the party was Archdeacon W. P. Johnson. He is still at work, and men in Africa still follow him anywhere. But he got bad ophthalmia and became quite blind for a time. He had to go back to England. The rest of the party pushed forward. After many delays and misadventures they arrived at Matope, far up the Shire river. There the plates of the steamer were to be riveted together, for the overland journey was over. The rest of the journey the steamer was to make by river and lake herself.

Ambali and the others set to work in earnest on that boat. They began very early in the morning. At eight o'clock, and again at noon, they stopped for food. Then they worked again till half-past five. Riveting is not light work in Central Africa, but at last it was finished. Then the coal bunkers were put in place. Fifteen men arrived with the mast for the boat. After that the deckboards were put on and the painting began. By mid-June, 1885, the shapeless pieces were built into a graceful little steamer almost ready to navigate the lake.

The machinery had still to be put together. In mid-August the riveting of the boiler began. A few days later there was a terrible fire. The engineer and a boy were at work within the boiler, over which a grass-covered shed had been raised to keep off the sun. As they worked, a little bit of red-hot rivet flew up and lodged in the grass roofing. It smouldered for a little and then blazed. The engineer, putting his head out of the boiler for a moment's fresh air, saw what had happened, and shouted " Fire ! "

The cry rang through the camp. Help came. The man-hole was at the top of the boiler, so it was not easy for those inside to get out. The boy went wild with fright. Water was thrown on the boiler to cool it. By the time the engineer and the boy were released the place was in a blaze.

Houses, stores, the carpenter's shop, a boat which had been beached in the shade, sails and ropes and cabin furniture for the steamer, all were on fire. Gunpowder and cartridges kept exploding. At last the flames leaped to the church, and that, too, was burned. Ambali, who had been helping to put out the fire, had nothing left but the shirt and cloth which he wore.

A few days later the little steamer, which the fire had not touched, was dedicated and named the *Charles Janson*, after a missionary who gave his life in Nyasaland. The Bishop in his robes and the Natives in their clean white garments walked in procession through the charred remains of the fire. The steamer was nearly ready to be launched. The Zanzibar carriers who had transported it had done their work, and Livingstone's old head man, Susi, led them overland on their long march home.

Now that only finishing touches were needed to complete the steamer, Ambali, three other teachers, and two white men went on in advance to Lake Nyasa. They travelled in an open sailing boat up the river and along the eastern shore of the lake. For twelve days they sailed, landing and making a little camp each night. Ambali noted the life of beast and bird and fish. But he did not enjoy the rough south wind which raised great waves to toss the heavy-laden boat. Nor was camping always to his mind. Lions roared horribly at night. A hippopotamus proved a restless neighbour. Thieves came and stole the anchor of the boat. Fever attacked the white men. But there was one happy night when the party found shelter on the bank of a small river and supped on fried goat's liver by moonlight.

Three days later they came to Likoma island, henceforth to be the headquarters of the diocese, and landed in St. Michael's Bay. Augustine Ambali had his share in the difficulties and adventures of settling on Likoma. Of these he tells in his book *Thirty Years in Nyasaland*. But his life work was not to be there, but on the mainland six miles away.

Among the Villages

The missionaries looked with longing on the villages across the belt of water from Likoma. There, on the low land between the lake and the hills, lay the clustered huts of the Nyanja people, some in large groups for mutual protection, some in small. Fear of two dread enemies drove the people to the edge of the lake. Down by the shore they were a little further from the wild and warlike Angoni, who made frequent raids to capture the Nyanja for slaves. The white ants were the other enemies. They came in their millions and ate up everything. But they did not like loose sand. It fell in and blocked their wonderful tunnels and checked their advance. So there the villages were, only a strip of water between them and the messengers who had brought good tidings about God.

There were few white men at Likoma. And none of the Zanzibar teachers was anxious to begin working in those villages across the lake. Augustine Ambali shrank from it as much as the rest. He hesitated, then he felt it was his duty, and he offered to go. With one of the white missionaries he spent a few months in pioneer work at Chia on the mainland. Then, being only a young teacher, he was sent back to Kiungani for further training. He travelled with Bishop Smythies. Two things in that journey the young man never forgot. One was the amazing energy of the Bishop, who walked far and " very, very fast " each day. The other was his gentleness and devotion. The people called him " the Native Bishop " because he loved them so much.

When Ambali had finished his period of study, he was admitted as a Reader. In August, 1888, he married a capable girl who had been educated in the mission and found in her a loving wife and unfailing helper. Then he and his bride, and a small party of which he was leader, took the long journey back to Likoma. In 1889 he began his life work in the villages on the eastern shore of the lake. At first he helped a white missionary. Then he went to

Zanzibar for more study, and was ordained, first deacon, and later on priest. After he had gained experience he was made priest in charge, with a staff of workers to help him. For twenty-eight years he worked in the Msumba district ; since 1918 he has been in charge of Ngoo Bay.

Msumba is a large village of about seven thousand inhabitants. Remnants of many tribes came together under one head chief that they might better withstand the Angoni. Work began under a tree in the open air. It grew and grew, amid difficulties and opposition, under the shepherding of Augustine Ambali. He visited ceaselessly and taught ; by his love for the people he weaned them from heathenism and trained them in the Christian way of life. He gathered boys round him, in school, in church, or for some outing among the mountains. Msumba became known as " the mother of teachers," so many from there went out into the work. Schools were opened, and little churches in outlying villages. There were many baptisms. The roll of communicants grew. Msumba was the centre of a living Christian Church. The Chief, Justus Amasanje, one of Ambali's pupils, became a sincere Christian.

After a time the needs of the work brought changes. Augustine Ambali was called in 1918 to leave Msumba and take up work at Ngoo Bay, some fifteen miles away. Simply and humbly he began again. He loved the second village as he had loved the first. He gathered fresh boys round him. He saw that the girls and infants had proper opportunities in school. He worked his simple dispensary. He visited the little churches and supervised the teachers in the villages round. All this and more he is doing in the year 1928. " I am an old man now," he says, " but I do my portion and leave the rest to others. My work is not done yet."

Augustine Ambali's life, so stirring in its beginnings, has been hidden among his villages for years. The Angoni were threatening at times, but things gradually settled down. The quiet uneventful years have been busy and full of peace. As the fragrance of flowers is carried far on the breeze so Augustine Ambali's fame has spread. Officials and travellers have heard of him and his work. When they meet him they feel his dignity and power. The white missionaries, men and women, trust and honour him and seek his counsel. New members of the mission gladly learn wisdom from his words and ways. He stands high in the councils of the Church. He is a Canon of Likoma, the first African Canon in the diocese. In the great gatherings of the mission his voice is listened to, his influence is felt.

Those who know the eastern coast of Lake Nyasa say that the shores are sandy with a fertile plain beyond, sometimes wide but usually narrow. Behind stand the hills, cut into beautiful valleys and clothed with a forest of small trees. These hills get a little brown in the dry season, but are always fair to see. The lake is exquisite, catching and reflecting the play and varying colour of the light. It is like, perhaps, the beauty which men love to watch in Augustine Ambali's life. There is little that is eventful or striking, but a heavenly light is over it all.

INDEX